The

STRANGE
UNSOLVED
MYSTERIES

VOLUME 2

**Strange Unsolved Mysteries
from Tor Books**

The Strangest of

STRANGE UNSOLVED MYSTERIES

VOLUME 2

Phyllis Raybin Emert

Illustrated by Jael

TOR®

A TOM DOHERTY ASSOCIATES BOOK
NEW YORK

THE STRANGEST OF STRANGE UNSOLVED MYSTERIES, VOLUME 2

Cover and interior art by Jael

A Tor Book
Published by Tom Doherty Associates, LLC
175 Fifth Avenue
New York, NY 10010

www.tor.com

Tor® is a registered trademark of Tom Doherty Associates, LLC.

ISBN-13: 978-0-7653-4191-4
ISBN-10: 0-7653-4191-3

First Edition: October 2002

Printed in the United States of America

0 9 8 7 6 5 4 3 2

For Jennifer Leigh Goldman
and the Sanders family:
Kelly Jane, Jeremy, Amy, Dawn, and Tom

Special Thanks to
the Fairfield Free Public Library
for assistance in researching
the illustrations

Contents

PART II: MYSTERIES OF BIZARRE ANIMALS AND FREAKS OF NATURE

Contents

The Strangest of

STRANGE UNSOLVED MYSTERIES

VOLUME 2

MYSTERIES OF PEOPLE and PLACES

Oak Island

The location of the buried treasure on Oak Island is a well-known fact. Only three-quarters of a mile long and half a mile wide, Oak Island lies in Mahone Bay off the coast of Nova Scotia, Canada. So why hasn't anyone claimed the treasure in nearly two hundred years? Many have tried, spending huge amounts of time and money in their search. Yet all have failed to solve the mystery of the "money pit."

It all started in 1795 when a young boy named Daniel McGinnis went exploring on Oak Island. Daniel came upon a large tree in a clearing and noticed a round, sunken area in the ground nearby. He also found the remains of what was once a road.

"It looks as if something's buried here," thought

Daniel. "Pirates used this island as a hideout years ago. Maybe it's the treasure of Blackbeard or Captain Kidd!"

Daniel returned the next morning with two friends. The three boys carried picks and shovels. They started to dig beneath the tree and uncovered a circle-shaped shaft. Four feet down, they found a layer of flagstones. Ten feet down, they came upon a platform of oak logs. This was definitely a man-made pit!

"Look," shouted Daniel as he held up his prize, "it's a rusty old ship's whistle!"

A few feet farther down, the boys discovered a copper coin with the date 1713.

"It won't be long now until we get to the treasure," Daniel declared.

At 20 feet there was another platform of oak logs. At 30 feet, they came upon still another platform.

This was only the beginning for Daniel McGinnis and his friends. They didn't give up on the treasure. Year after year, they dug in the pit whenever they had free time.

As they grew older, two of the boys married and brought their brides to live on Oak Island so that they could remain close to the treasure. Daniel and his friends were sure that they would someday reach their goal.

In 1804, a wealthy man named Dr. John Lynds joined in the search for the treasure. But every 10 feet they dug, the workers hit another platform of oak logs.

Deeper and deeper they dug. At 93 feet, they discovered layers of charcoal, putty, and coconut fiber. The fiber was definitely brought to the island from somewhere else, since it couldn't be found locally. Next, they found a large, flat tablet covered with markings that looked like writing.

It has been said that the markings were later deciphered to read "Two million pounds be buried 10 feet below." But many are doubtful that this is the true meaning.

At 95 feet, the hole mysteriously filled with 60 feet of water. A second shaft dug next to the original also filled with water, and the digging had to be stopped.

Another group tried again in 1849. This time they used a pod auger drill to dig deeper into the original shaft. At 98 feet, the drill went through what was believed to be the treasure chamber, and the workers discovered three gold links from a chain. But the constant flow of water prevented them from bringing up the treasure.

The treasure hunters found that the water was flowing in from the ocean at nearby Smith's Cove. A seawater channel had been dug by whoever buried the treasure to prevent people from taking it!

Over the years, more digging expeditions were attempted. Although these also failed, more was discovered about the money pit. The treasure chests at 98 feet were just a portion of the riches. A cement chamber uncovered at 151 feet was thought to hold the real treasure.

As digging continued, a second seawater channel that protected the treasure was discovered. A piece of parchment with letters on it was brought up by a drill in 1893. An iron plate was discovered in place 170 feet down.

Attempts were made to stop the flow of water from the ocean. Hundreds of thousands of dollars were spent, but nothing was successful. After so much digging, the pit eventually became such a mass of slippery mud that the original shaft and treasure chests couldn't even be located.

To this day, the treasure is still waiting to be taken. How much is it worth? Who put it there? These questions remain unanswered. Many people feel it must be an extremely valuable treasure for someone to have gone to the trouble of protecting it in such a complicated way.

Many believe a pirate or group of pirates buried the treasure on Oak Island. Captain William Kidd has often been linked to the money pit. Others say a French army pay ship concealed the treasure to hide it from the British.

One thing is certain: a large number of men must have worked for a long time to build the elaborate seawater system that protects the treasure. But how could even the designer of the money pit then come back to claim the treasure? It is believed that there was some type of secret gate or dam system that shut off the ocean water. But no one knows where this is located or how it might work.

Expert engineers are convinced that with modern equipment and unlimited financing, the treasure could easily be located, but that has been said many times before.

Will the mystery of the money pit ever be solved? No one knows. The challenge of the unknown and the possibility of great wealth continue to fascinate treasure seekers everywhere.

Fire from Nowhere

The weekly dance at the Chelmsford Shire Hall in England was just ending on August 27, 1938. It was midnight, and Phyllis Newcombe had spent the evening dancing with her fiancé, Henry McAusland. She was wearing a lovely, full-skirted crinoline dress, perfect for showing off her superior dancing skills.

As the couple stepped off the dance floor, the beautiful dress suddenly burst into flames. Within seconds, the screaming twenty-two-year-old was engulfed by fire!

Henry tried to beat the flames out with his hands, but it was no use. Other couples stood watching, paralyzed by fear and shock. Within a mere two minutes, Phyllis had been reduced to "a blackened mass of ash!"

How could such a thing happen? At the court hearing, the coroner concluded that a lit cigarette had accidentally set the dress on fire, thus causing the horrible death of Phyllis Newcombe.

But Phyllis's father was not convinced. He held up a piece of material from his late daughter's dress and challenged the coroner to set it on fire.

"Use this," he said, handing the coroner a lit cigarette.

Try as he might, the coroner could not set the material on fire with the cigarette.

"All the witnesses to my daughter's death at the dance swore they had no cigarettes of any kind," declared Mr. Newcombe.

The mysterious case of Phyllis Newcombe is just one of dozens of unexplained cases in which people have burst into flames for no apparent reason. Some people call this phenomenon spontaneous human combustion, or SHC. It is defined as "a fire whose origins cannot be stated with certainty."

Most victims of SHC are totally destroyed by the fire. Although hands and feet may escape the flames, the trunk of the body is usually reduced to ashes. Oftentimes furniture or even the victim's clothes are hardly damaged. In most cases, the victims have been discovered in their homes (or even cars) totally burned. Yet their chair, couch, bed, automobile, or clothing remained intact.

To totally burn a human body to ashes, a temperature of about 1,700 degrees Fahrenheit over a period of at least ninety minutes is required.

Some believe that in SHC the fire comes from

within the individual. It is triggered in a rare number of people when a powerful energy or current is released, the result being an eruption of flames. Is SHC a short circuiting of the body's energy forces? No one knows for sure.

There are those who believe that there is no such thing as SHC. They argue that these burnings occurred as a result of external fires started from cigarette or pipe ash, or embers from a fireplace. The fat naturally present in the human body liquefies and adds fuel to the fire, causing complete incineration.

Many scientists say that a logical explanation for incidents of SHC may have been overlooked. The challenge for them is to find the real cause of the fire.

Is SHC a short circuiting of bodily energy, or are there other reasons for these strange and mysterious incidents? You be the judge.

Explosion in Siberia

A blazing fireball, brighter than the morning sun, raced across the sky on June 30, 1908. A thunderous boom and powerful wind panicked the small population of villagers in remote central Russia. Trees and buildings were flattened. The fireball hit the ground with such force that strong vibrations were recorded thousands of miles away.

Upon the fireball's impact, the sky exploded into fire and deafening thunder. A heat wave, followed by a shock wave, raced across the wilderness, destroying everything in their paths and causing fires. Black rain and more thunder followed.

It happened at the Stony Tunguska River in Siberia, Russia, more than eighty-three years ago. Scientists believe it to be the greatest explosion that ever took place on Earth, more powerful than the atom bombs dropped on Japan in World War II!

For weeks after the blast, there were changes in the Earth's magnetic field and atmosphere. People noticed unusually odd and colorful lights in the sky. Over Siberia and parts of Europe, strange silver clouds gave off so much light that it was possible to read a book at all hours and even take photographs at midnight without using a flash.

The explosion attracted little attention because Siberia occupied a huge area of land and its population was small and isolated. From 1908 to 1921, there was no known investigation of any kind into what had happened in this remote place. When expeditions to the site of the explosion began later in the 1920s, researchers found that the cold climate and frozen ground had preserved the aftereffects of the blast.

Many scientists believed a large meteor had fallen, yet no meteor crater could be found. Instead, thousands of uprooted, flattened, and scorched trees lay everywhere, and "the solid ground heaved outward . . . like waves in water." Scientists wondered if a meteor had exploded in the air above the ground.

After World War II, a Russian scientist compared the Siberian explosion in 1908 to the aftereffects of the atomic bomb dropped on Hiroshima, Japan, in 1945. He had visited both places and found too many similarities to believe it was simply a coincidence.

Could the 1908 blast have been an atomic explo-

sion? The development of the bomb didn't even begin until the late 1930s. Could it have come from someplace other than Earth? Was the blazing fireball an out-of-control alien spaceship that used atomic fuel?

Although many discount this theory, certain facts cannot be ignored. Witnesses in 1908 saw a blazing fireball and a flash of light. They then experienced a thermal (heat) wave and a fire storm. This was followed by a powerful shock wave and black rain. These are the very things seen and experienced by survivors of the Hiroshima and Nagasaki A-bomb blasts in 1945.

In 1959, a Russian expedition tested soil and plants in the Stony Tunguska River area. Even fifty-one years after the blast, they found radiation levels double those in other areas. Few lives were lost from radiation sickness in 1908 because the area of the explosion was a remote wilderness, unlike the densely populated Japanese cities that were hit in 1945.

All evidence points to a high-altitude atomic explosion. A few scientists believe that the explosion in Siberia was fifteen hundred times larger than that of the Hiroshima bomb. But what was the cause of the blast?

Witnesses in 1908 said the fireball looked cylindrical in shape, like a pipe or tube. Was it a spaceship from another world? Some people think so.

Within the Milky Way galaxy (which is one of the millions of galaxies in the universe), there are millions of suns and planetary systems like our own. With so many possibilities, aren't there bound to be some planets like Earth that are home to intelligent life forms?

On March 3, 1972, an unmanned space probe called Pioneer 10 was launched into space by the United States. It flew over Jupiter, then left the solar system for deep space. Attached to Pioneer 10 was an aluminum plaque with human figures engraved on it, along with a message for extraterrestrial beings!

Could a spacecraft from another world, fueled by atomic power, have entered the Earth's atmosphere in 1908? Could something have gone wrong, causing the craft to explode over the Stony Tunguska River?

The existence of the ship and the possible life forms within it are gone forever. What remains are detailed records of a huge explosion and an immense area of destruction. But without actual proof, the cause of the blast in Siberia will remain an unsolved mystery.

Jack the Ripper

The murders began on Friday, August 31, 1888, in the Whitechapel area of London, England.

The first victim was Mary Ann Nichols. "No murder was ever more ferociously and more brutally done," according to the *Star* newspaper.

When Annie Chapman's body was discovered eight days later, the police knew they had a madman on their hands. But he was also a killer who had some degree of medical know-how and a thorough knowledge of human anatomy. They decided this was someone who was very skilled with a knife.

People began to panic after the second murder, but the police didn't have any clues. On September 25, the killer wrote a letter to the Central News Agency: "I keep hearing the police have caught me but they won't fix me just yet." It was signed, "Yours truly, Jack the Ripper."

The murder victims lived in the East End slums of London. It was a tough area, home to the poor and the sick. There were always fights and many crimes in this neighborhood, and murder was fairly common.

The Ripper's victims were poor, drunken women who made their living on the streets. His crimes were so brutal that even upper-class people were disturbed by them. But in the East End, people were terrified.

"Double event this time," boasted Jack in another letter to the press. On September 30, Elizabeth Stride and Catherine Eddowes became victims numbers three and four.

People were outraged when they read of the murders. "What are the police doing?" they asked. "Scotland Yard has got to do something!"

Errors were made during the investigation. Evidence was washed away by mistake. Clues were overlooked. The police made dozens of arrests, but all suspects were released when leads proved to be false.

Mary Jane Kelly became victim number five on November 9, 1888. She was murdered inside her apartment, not on the street like the others. "It looked like the work of a devil," said one witness.

Queen Victoria called for a special investigation. The Prime Minister, Lord Salisbury, held a special meeting of the cabinet to discuss the sensational Ripper case.

Everyone had his or her own idea as to the identity of the killer. Was it a butcher who worked in one of London's slaughterhouses? Could it be a mad doctor or surgeon from London Hospital, which was located on Whitechapel Road?

Some people believed that Jack wasn't a man at all. Perhaps the Ripper was a woman, or even a policeman. In later years, suspicion was cast upon the royal family itself. Could the mad killer have been Edward, the Duke of Clarence, the grandson of Queen Victoria?

With the death of Mary Jane Kelly, the Ripper murders ended. It was almost as if Jack himself vanished from London. Some believe the killer committed suicide. Others say he left the city and continued his awful crimes in other parts of the world.

One modern movie, *Time After Time*, even suggested that Jack was a respected doctor and a friend of inventor and author H. G. Wells. In the film, Jack uses Wells's time machine to travel into the future and continues to murder innocent female victims.

Some people have questioned whether Jack's letters to the press were real or fake. Did a reporter make them up to increase newspaper sales, or were they written by the crazed Ripper himself?

The basic fact remains that Jack the Ripper was never caught, and his identity, 103 years later, is still an unexplained mystery.

The *Royal Charter*

"The wind is changing direction, Captain!" shouted the first mate of the British clipper ship the *Royal Charter*. "It's forcing us back!" he screamed, hoping to be heard above the storm.

"God help us, we're drifting toward the rocks offshore," cried the captain. "Full steam power, roll in the sails!" he ordered. "Drop the anchors!"

Gale-force winds up to sixty-three miles per hour began to tear the sails apart. The small steam engine couldn't stop the ship's deadly drift.

It was October 1859, and the 2,700-ton *Royal Charter* was on the last leg of its long voyage home from Australia to Liverpool, England. Powered by steam and sails, the *Royal Charter* carried a 322,000-pound cargo of gold bars, gold dust, and gold coins. Many of the five hundred passengers on board were successful gold prospectors who carried their own personal fortunes from the gold-fields of Australia.

The *Royal Charter* started to break up on the rocks off the east coast of Anglesey, north of Wales. Wave upon wave smashed over the helpless ship as its sails became tangled in its propeller.

Local residents rushed to the shore to help, but lifeboats were useless in the wind and waves. Suddenly the ship broke completely in two. Hundreds of passengers and the valuable cargo were thrown into the violent sea.

Men tried to swim to shore, their pockets stuffed with gold nuggets that weighed them down. They drowned rather than give up their gold. Others perished because they didn't know how to swim. Many of the women refused to take off their outer clothes and swim to safety because they were too shy. They jumped into the churning water fully dressed. The layers of clothing weighed them down and they, too, lost their lives.

A total of 459 people died on the *Royal Charter* that horrible day. Bodies were smashed and torn-up on the rocks, and gold was tossed everywhere. The power of the waves was so strong that one large bar of gold was later found driven deep into a piece of solid iron!

In the year following the *Royal Charter* disaster, divers managed to bring up much of the solid gold valuables from the wreck. But a large quantity remains on the ocean floor off Anglesey to this day.

A memorial has been built on the site of the

wreck, and treasure hunters continue to be drawn to the spot. In 1958, two divers were exploring the underwater remains of the clipper ship when they came upon a large gold bar sticking up out of the sand. The two tried to free the bar, but it was jammed between two pieces of twisted metal. The divers ran out of air and had to surface before they could free it.

It was three days before they could get new compressed-air cylinders for another dive. A storm came up, making the delay even longer. When the divers finally went back into the water to recover their fortune, they were shocked to find that the storm had changed the bottom of the ocean floor, and sand now covered much of the wreck. The men couldn't find the gold bar!

In 1985, a diving team brought up several gold coins, nuggets, and other items from the wreck, but much of the treasure still remains off the Anglesey coast, close to shore. Each new storm causes movement and changes on the ocean floor that present many challenges and opportunities for treasure hunters.

Who knows how much gold lies waiting to be discovered in and around the wreck of the *Royal Charter*? More than 130 years have passed, and the gold still waits patiently to be rediscovered.

The Masked Man

Alexandre Dumas wrote about an imprisoned man in his popular book *The Man in the Iron Mask*. The mysterious prisoner wore "a visor of polished steel which enveloped the whole of his head."

In the Dumas novel, the prisoner is the half-brother of King Louis XIV of France. He looked so much like the king that the king felt he was a threat to the crown and could not be allowed to remain free.

There really was a masked prisoner, but he was never fitted with an iron mask. For years he wore a mask of black velvet. His true identity remains a mystery even to this day.

Louis XIV was king of France for seventy-two years (1643–1715), the longest reign in history. He became king at the age of five. He was a very powerful ruler and once declared, "I am the State."

His subjects called him the Sun King because of the brilliance of his court. Everything in France revolved around Louis, who believed he answered only to God.

Throughout the years of his reign, many people were imprisoned by the king for various political and personal crimes. No one questioned the Sun King's motives or reasons. Most jailers simply followed his orders.

But this prisoner was different. The king seemed to be concerned that he be treated well and allowed him certain special privileges. On July 19, 1669, a note from the Minister of War, the Marquis de Louvois, was sent to Monsieur de Saint-Mars, commander of the Pignerol Prison. In the note, the prisoner is mentioned for the first and only time by the name of Eustache Dauger, which means "to stab" or "hollow out" in French. Many believe it was a false name.

The note explained how the prisoner should be treated. He was to be completely isolated from others and not allowed to talk to anyone. He was to be treated politely and given as many prayer books as he wanted.

The prisoner was allowed to hear Mass on Sundays and have a priest for confession several times a year. He was also given musical instruments to play. Obviously this was not an ordinary prisoner! The question is, who was he?

The prisoner remained at Pignerol from 1669 to

1678. He then accompanied Saint-Mars to the prison at Saint Marguerite and stayed there for twenty years. In all this time, he was never again referred to as Eustache Dauger, and he never wore a mask. Any contact the prisoner had with others was always through a curtain or behind a door.

In 1698, Saint-Mars became the governor of the Bastille Prison in Paris. The man, now called the "Ancient Prisoner," was transferred there. But this time the tall, white-haired prisoner was marched into the Bastille tower wearing a black velvet mask!

The masked man remained alive for five more years. When he died on November 19, 1703, he was buried in the churchyard under another false name. Even in death, his identity was kept a secret.

During the thirty-four years of his imprisonment, the man hardly spoke and was a model inmate. Fifty years later, the French novelist Voltaire wrote about an incident that occurred while the prisoner was at Saint Marguerite Prison. According to Voltaire, "the prisoner wrote something with his knife on a silver plate and threw it out the window."

A fisherman picked up the plate and returned it to Saint-Mars, who lifted his pistol to the man's head and asked him if he had read the message. "I can't read," the fisherman replied. "Then you're a lucky man," said Saint-Mars, putting down his pistol. "You're free to go."

Many people were curious about the mysterious prisoner when he was alive in seventeenth-century France. Interest increased after his death. Who was

he? Why was he treated so well by the king, yet kept imprisoned for so many years? Why didn't Louis XIV want him to be recognized? If the prisoner was such a threat to the Sun King, why hadn't he been executed? Perhaps he was related to Louis in some way, which would explain the special treatment.

Could Alexandre Dumas have been right? Was the prisoner a half- or twin brother who looked just like the king and was therefore too dangerous to be set free or recognized? They were similar in age. But wouldn't a look-alike already have been well known and recognized by the time of his arrest?

A man named Eustache D'Auger, the nearly identical name given to the prisoner in 1669, really did exist. He was involved with the notorious Marquise de Brinvilliers, a convicted murderess. She was executed after being found guilty of poisoning eighteen people.

Years before, D'Auger had apparently assisted her in several Black Mass devil worship celebrations. Was this D'Auger the same man imprisoned for thirty-four years? If so, why go to such trouble to keep his identity a mystery? Surely a devil worshiper would not have been treated so kindly by the king. Did the mystery man have some sort of hold over the king? Why wasn't D'Auger executed?

More than three hundred years have passed, and still the identity of the masked prisoner remains a mystery. Perhaps someday the missing piece to the puzzle will be found.

Winchester House

They called the Winchester repeating rifle "the gun that won the West." For Sarah Pardee Winchester, that gun put a curse on her life.

Following the death of her husband, William Wirt Winchester, Sarah inherited the Winchester family fortune. She was left $20 million.

"The spirits of all those killed by the Winchester rifle will haunt you forever," a Boston psychic told Sarah. The psychic supposedly communicated with the dead. "Your money is cursed. The spirits are after you," explained the psychic. "You must build a large house to please them."

Believing what she was told, Sarah moved west to California in 1884 and purchased an eight-room house on a large lot in San Jose. Expansion of the house began immediately and construction didn't end until thirty-eight years later, when she died!

Sarah hired more than twenty full-time carpenters and masons, who worked seven days a week around the clock to add new rooms to the house. She employed twelve to eighteen gardeners to tend the many acres of grounds.

Sarah believed she could escape from and frustrate the evil spirits through hiding and trickery. She built stairways to nowhere, dead-end corridors, and windows that looked out onto walls. She created secret passageways, sealed off rooms, and slept in a different bedroom each night.

To please the good spirits, Sarah bought only the most expensive furniture for her mansion. Workmen used the finest materials in laying the floors and wallpapering the rooms. Gold, silver, and precious jewels were embedded in the doors and windows.

A large bell tower was built with no doors. Only two servants knew the exact location of the underground passageway that led to the huge bell. Each evening at midnight and 2 A.M. the bell was rung. These were the hours when Sarah visited her secret "blue room."

In the blue room, she communicated with the good spirits who instructed her in the building of the house. Only Sarah knew the way to this room through secret panels and windows that led to mazes of stairways.

More than a hundred rooms were added to the house. Forty-seven chimneys were built, as well as three working elevators. Some hallways were very

jael

narrow and some ceilings very low. One room was full of different-sized balconies. Many doors, once closed, would not open again from the inside of the room.

The grand ballroom was completely hand-carved and constructed without nails, at a cost of nine thousand dollars. The stained-glass window alone cost two thousand dollars.

Gold and silver decorated the walls of the dining hall. Night after night, Sarah sat at the head of the table in formal dress. Twelve other places were set so the good spirits could dine with her. The best chefs in the world served Sarah and her spirit friends the most expensive gourmet foods on plates of gold.

The number 13 was used in the Winchester mansion as often as possible. There were thirteen bathrooms. Many rooms had thirteen windows and doors. The chandeliers each had thirteen lights. The stairways had thirteen steps. Thirteen palm trees lined the driveway, and there were thirteen drain holes in the kitchen sink. Even Sarah's will had thirteen parts, and she signed it thirteen times!

Sarah Winchester died in 1922 at the age of 85. When word came of her death, all construction on the house stopped immediately. It is estimated that she spent $5.5 million trying to please the spirits.

Today the 150-room mansion is open to visitors, and many of them have reported strange incidents. Some see moving lights or feel wind and cold spots. Others hear footsteps and whispers. Doors and windows mysteriously open and close by themselves.

Is it their imagination? Or does the spirit of Sarah Winchester live on in her strange house?

Dorothy Arnold

December 12, 1910, seemed like a typical day in the life of twenty-five-year-old Dorothy Arnold. That morning she dressed to go out shopping. She wore a long blue coat over a skirt. The coat hung down to her ankles. Her high-button shoes reached up to her calves.

Dorothy wore a large hat, carried a satin purse, and kept her hands warm in a silver-fox muff. Anyone looking at her would know she was a fashionable woman from a wealthy family.

Dorothy's father, Francis Arnold, was a successful businessman whose ancestors had arrived on the *Mayflower*. Her uncle was a member of the U.S. Supreme Court.

"I'm going shopping, Mother," announced Dorothy. "I need an evening dress for Marjorie's coming-out party. It's only five days away." Marjorie was Dorothy's younger sister.

"Maybe I'd better go with you," replied Mrs. Arnold.

"No, Mother. Don't bother," answered Dorothy. "I might not see a thing I want, but if I do, I'll phone you."

That was the last conversation Mrs. Arnold ever had with her daughter!

Dorothy left her home on Seventy-ninth Street in Manhattan at 11 A.M. She took with her about thirty-six dollars from the bank and her twenty-five-dollar monthly allowance. Turning onto Fifth Avenue, she walked twenty blocks over icy sidewalks to a candy store. There Dorothy bought a half-pound box of chocolates.

Thirty-two blocks later she reached Brentano's bookstore. There she bought a book called *An Engaged Girl's Sketches* by Emily Calvin Blake.

Outside the bookstore, Dorothy met a friend named Gladys King. They talked for a while about Marjorie's coming-out party, then the girls said good-bye. It was about 2 P.M. and Gladys turned to wave one last time at Dorothy. After that she was never seen again!

When Dorothy didn't come home that night, the Arnolds hired their own private detective to find her. Why didn't they notify the police? The wealthy family didn't want any bad publicity. In fact, Mr. Arnold lied and told one of Dorothy's friends that she had come home. It wasn't until six weeks later that the police were called!

Mr. Arnold believed that Dorothy had been murdered in Central Park on her walk home and that her body had been thrown in the reservoir. But no body or trace of violence was ever found.

Could Dorothy have arranged her own disappearance? She was a happy, well-adjusted young woman . . . or was she? In the months following her disappearance, certain surprising facts came to light.

Against her father's wishes and without his knowledge, Dorothy was dating a man named George Griscom, Jr. "Junior," as he was called, was over forty, bald, fat, and unemployed, but Dorothy seemed to be in love. She even spent a secret weekend with him in Boston. Junior was in Italy when Dorothy disappeared and claimed he had no idea what had happened to her.

Months before, Dorothy told her father she wanted to move to Greenwich Village and become a writer. Mr. Arnold was totally opposed to his daughter's living on her own.

When two of Dorothy's short stories were rejected for publication by *McClure's* magazine, the family teased Dorothy about it. She was so disturbed that she rented her own mailbox so the family wouldn't know about her writing career.

In a letter to Junior in Italy, Dorothy wrote, "*McClure's* has turned me down. All I can see ahead is a long road with no turning. Mother will always think an accident has happened."

What did she mean by "an accident has happened"? Did Dorothy plan to take her own life? Or did she want to run away from the family?

Directly after her disappearance, the private detective found two steamship folders on her desk. Did Dorothy take an ocean voyage under another name and start a new life somewhere else? Or were those folders left purposely on her desk to confuse those who searched for her?

Was she planning to meet Junior in Europe? If so, she never did. He returned to the United States and placed ads in newspapers begging Dorothy to come back to him.

Did Dorothy Arnold run away? Was it suicide or murder? Some people believe the Arnold family knew more about what happened to their daughter than they let on. Were they covering up something that might cause an unwanted scandal?

No trace of Dorothy Arnold was ever found. Her fate remains a mystery.

The Dragon's Triangle

"The *Derbyshire* is a jinxed ship," wrote crewman Peter Lambert to his mother in Liverpool, England. "There have been too many accidents on board. Strange things are happening! I won't sail on the *Derbyshire* again," he added.

In September 1980, Peter Lambert was one of a forty-four-man crew that disappeared when the huge ship weighing almost 170,000 tons went down south of Tokyo Bay, Japan. No calls for help were heard over the radio.

Whatever happened to the *Derbyshire* was sudden and overwhelming. Officials believe that a severe, unexpected storm of high waves and winds broke the long, narrow ship in half. Not a trace of the *Derbyshire* or its crew was found!

The area in which the ship went down is located

in the Pacific Ocean between Japan, the Philippines, and the Marianas Islands. It is called the Dragon's Triangle. Hundreds of small boats, dozens of larger vessels, and even Soviet nuclear-powered submarines have vanished there.

Strange disappearances haven't been limited to seagoing vessels. Numerous airplanes have also vanished. In 1945 during the last days of World War II, a Japanese Kawanishi flying boat was on patrol near Iwo Jima in the Pacific. The last message sent before the plane disappeared forever was spoken by the pilot. He said, "Something is happening to the sky . . . the sky is opening up." The weather was good and there were no combat attacks that night.

March of 1957 was a memorable month in the Dragon's Triangle. In a nine-day period, three planes disappeared suddenly and without explanation. On March 12, a KB-50 tanker vanished with a crew of eight on a routine flight from Japan to Wake Island. A U.S. Navy JD-1 Invader disappeared between Japan and Okinawa on March 16. Six days later, on March 22, a U.S. military transport vanished southeast of Japan.

A total of eighty lives were lost in the three disappearances. In each case, the weather was clear, no SOS calls were ever received, and no trace of the planes or crews was ever found!

The Japanese call this area of the Pacific "the Sea of the Devil." Some seamen believe that dragons and demons are responsible for the disappearances in the area.

Many of the deepest ocean trenches in the world are located in the Dragon's Triangle. The Mariana Trench is 36,190 feet deep—that's nearly seven miles straight down! Who knows what powerful forces or even sea creatures are located at such depths?

Some believe the area of the Dragon's Triangle is prone to changes in the Earth's magnetic field, which could affect a ship's or plane's sensitive instruments. Others suggest natural causes such as underwater earthquakes, which could produce sudden, violent waves on the surface of the ocean. Undersea volcanic activity could result in dangerous surface conditions. Sudden violent storms, thunderous waves, and wind-shear downdrafts are also very hazardous to both air and sea traffic.

For some unexplained reason, sightings of unidentified flying objects, or UFOs, are high in the area of the Dragon's Triangle. Could there be a connection between these sightings and the disappearances of so many ships and planes?

Scientists believe that areas of massive energy called black holes exist in outer space. Are they gateways to other worlds? Could there be areas similar to black holes in the ocean depths of the Dragon's Triangle?

There are no definite answers to these questions. Until there is more proof, the Dragon's Triangle remains a mystery. Enter it at your own risk!

Harry Houdini

"How does he do it?" asked one woman in the audience.

"It's impossible. He's going to drown in there!" declared a worried man.

"No human being can escape from there," exclaimed another. "He must have special powers different from those of ordinary men."

"Harry Houdini is not ordinary!" another woman added.

The stunt was called the Chinese Water Torture Cell and described as "a feat which borders on the supernatural." Houdini offered one thousand dollars to anyone who could prove it was possible to breathe in the water-filled compartment from which he escaped.

A metal-lined mahogany tank was filled with

water. It had a plate of glass in front so the audience could see inside. Then a metal cage was put into the tank. With his ankles locked in place, Houdini was lowered headfirst into the water tank, and the top was securely locked.

The audience clearly saw Houdini upside down in the cage inside the water tank. Assistants placed a curtained screen around the tank and stood nearby holding axes, ready to break the glass in case of an emergency.

Seconds passed as the audience waited. After a minute, the assistants checked their watches. After ninety seconds, the audience squirmed in their seats. When the two-minute mark passed, the assistants raised their axes.

Suddenly, the curtains parted. Out stepped Houdini, soaking wet and smiling. Behind him, the tank was still filled with water, and locked just as before!

Harry Houdini, born Erich Weiss, was an extraordinary athlete and a master magician. He could do things with his body that others wouldn't even dream of.

While upside down in the Water Torture Cell, Houdini was able to double himself up and pick the lock that held his feet. Then he stood upright and unlocked the top of the tank, all the while holding his breath. He hauled himself out and snapped the locks back into place.

There were few locks in the world that Houdini's sensitive fingers couldn't manipulate. But this skill came only after years of studying and designing locks. He gained his early fame as the "Hand-cuff King" by challenging police departments in various cities to lock him up. Even the handcuffs of England's Scotland Yard couldn't hold Hou-dini!

Many of his stunts involved escaping from impossible situations while under water. He was an excellent swimmer and trained himself to hold his breath for more than four minutes at a time. Few could match this expert at breath control.

Houdini often sat in ice water to get his body used to intense cold. In the dead of winter he jumped off bridges into rivers, chained and hand-cuffed. Sometimes he was placed, chained and cuffed, into a barrel or other container that was then nailed shut and lowered into the water.

There was always the risk that something could go wrong in one of these stunts and he might drown. But Houdini never panicked. He once declared, "Fear is fatal."

Though many actually believed Houdini had mysterious powers, he scoffed at the notion. He was proud of his physical conditioning and muscular abilities.

As an aid to other magicians, Houdini wrote detailed descriptions of how he did all of his stunts. He invented a small picklock that he hid in his mouth or body to help free himself. He could use his toes as fingers, and he could even spring a lock with his teeth!

Most of the containers Houdini used had a trick panel that gave way a little and allowed him to slip

through. He was incredibly strong and flexible and could wriggle through the smallest openings.

Once Houdini was wrapped in a straitjacket and hung upside down in front of Keith's Theatre in Washington, D.C. No tools were used in these straitjacket escapes. His excellent physical condition and muscle control allowed him to escape within minutes.

Many say Harry Houdini was the greatest magician of all time. He once told his wife that after he died, he would find a way to communicate with her from the grave. He died on Halloween of 1926, at the age of fifty-two. His wife, Bess, waited years for his message, but it never came.

The mystery of Harry Houdini isn't in the magic of his remarkable stunts. The mystery is how he used discipline and self-control to train his body to do things so incredible that no magician has been able to duplicate them since.

Easter Island

Huge stone faces with large noses and long ears are found everywhere on Easter Island. They are called *moai*.

Once, long ago, six hundred enormous statues, from ten to forty feet high, stood along the coast or at sacred burial sites. There were giant heads along the roads and at the inactive volcano, Rano Raraku, where they were carved.

Easter Island is located in the South Pacific, 2,200 miles west of Chile. The nearest inhabited island is 1,200 miles away. First discovered by Dutch explorer Jacob Roggeveen in 1722, the small island was named in honor of the Easter holiday. Roggeveen and his crew marveled at the stone heads. Most were topped with what looked like tall red hats or crowns and sat on stone platforms.

Today, most of the heads are toppled over and lie facedown in the dirt. Many are broken at the neck. More than two hundred still lie on the ground, unfinished, gazing up at the sky in the volcano quarry. The largest of these is sixty-nine feet long!

Islanders used hand picks to carve the rock into a statue. The picks are scattered everywhere on the ground. It is as if the stone carvers suddenly put down their tools and left forever!

Years passed and Easter Island was forgotten. Then ships from different nations visited the area. In 1774, Captain James Cook wrote in detail about the people, customs, and government of the island. By this time, most of the stone faces had been mysteriously pulled down.

In 1862, South American slave traders captured one thousand islanders, including the king and his son. They were forced to work on the islands off the coast of Chile. Many died and only fifteen lived to return to their homeland. Those who did brought with them a smallpox epidemic. By 1877, only about one hundred people were left on Easter Island.

These survivors and their descendants are all that remain of the original culture. Today, about twenty-five hundred people live on Easter Island. Annexed by Chile in 1888, the people speak Spanish and Rapa Nui, a Polynesian language.

The giant stone faces have mystified everyone since their discovery 270 years ago. Sculptors carved them out of volcanic rock with stone picks.

But for many years, people wondered how such heavy objects were moved to different parts of the island.

It was found that natives used sleds made from the stems of banana trees to transport the *moai*, and they pulled them with ropes of hemp fiber. They used levers to raise the statues a little at a time, then placed small stones under them. As the stone piles gradually grew, the statues rose off the ground and stood upright.

Most of the *moai* were placed near 250 burial platforms, called *ahu*, and were built to honor their respected ancestors. The *ahu moai* have topknots and eyes made of white coral or red volcanic rock.

There are several theories that attempt to explain many of the mysteries surrounding Easter Island, such as where did the original islanders come from? What happened between 1722 and 1774 to cause them to destroy the statues they took so long to make?

Most believe the ancestors of the Easter Islanders were Polynesians who originally came from southeast Asia. They traveled across the ocean and settled on many islands in the Pacific.

However, anthropologist Thor Heyerdahl of Norway believes that they came from South America, not Asia. He thinks the white men from Peru had an influence on the development of culture on Easter Island.

In two separate waves of migration (about A.D. 380 and A.D. 1100), Peruvians arrived on Easter Island and used their stone-carving skills. Then around

A.D. 1400, Polynesians arrived, and eventually war broke out between the two groups. The war between the Polynesians (the short ears) and the Peruvian stone carvers (the long ears) resulted in the massacre of the long ears and the pulling down of all the statues. The victorious short ears practiced cannibalism and ate the losers.

Local legends support Heyerdahl's theory. They mention war between groups on the island. Different families or tribes, each with their own *ahu*, fought and killed one another, overturning the *moai*.

But one mystery remains. Why did work on the stone statues stop so suddenly? Why were so many *moai* left unfinished at the volcano quarry, as if all the workers dropped their tools abruptly and departed?

Could the islanders have lost interest in statue carving all at once? Did everyone rush to fight and protect his family when war broke out? Was there a terrible catastrophe or natural phenomenon such as a lunar or solar eclipse that frightened them? No one knows for sure.

D. B. Cooper

The last passenger to board Northwest Airlines Flight 305 was a tall, dark, middle-aged man. He carried a black briefcase and sat in the last row on the right side.

"Dan Cooper" was the name he gave to the flight attendant. The Boeing 727 was on its way to Seattle, Washington, from Portland, Oregon. There were only thirty-six passengers aboard the thirty-minute flight. It was November 24, 1971, the day before Thanksgiving.

Passenger Cooper ordered two drinks. When the flight attendant gave him his change, Cooper handed her a white envelope. "Take it," he said.

The flight attendant, Florence Schaffner, took the envelope and started to put it into her pocket. "Read it now," the man insisted.

Florence opened the envelope and read the note inside. "I have a bomb in my briefcase," the note said. "I will use it if necessary. I want you to sit next to me. You are being hijacked."

Is this guy kidding? thought Florence. But she noticed the black briefcase and did as she was told. Cooper opened the case to reveal a number of red sticks connected to wire. Was it dynamite?

"He can really blow up the plane!" thought Florence, alarmed. She waited as Cooper wrote a demand note. He asked for $200,000 in used $20 bills, as well as two back and two chest parachutes.

Taking no chances, Northwest Airlines decided to meet the demands of the hijacker. The money and parachutes were delivered to the plane in Seattle and the passengers were freed after refueling. The 727 took off again that evening and headed south. Only the crew and Cooper were aboard.

"Don't fly higher than ten thousand feet or faster than two hundred miles per hour," he ordered.

Cooper forced the crew into the front cabin, then retreated to the rear of the plane. "He's planning to jump now," the captain declared.

"He must be crazy," said one of the flight attendants. "We're flying through freezing rain, with wind gusts up to seventy miles per hour, and sub-zero temperatures. And he's only wearing a normal suit and raincoat."

The airplane shuddered as the unlocked rear-cabin door opened to the outside. "He must be jumping right now," said the captain. It was 8:13 P.M. Below the plane lay the wilderness of southwest Washington state.

Despite an extensive search, not a trace of Dan Cooper, his clothing, or the parachutes was ever seen again!

How did the extra initial get stuck to Dan Cooper's name? A reporter made an error in a news story, and the other papers picked up the mistake. Dan Cooper became D. B. Cooper, and he made the FBI's 10 Most Wanted List!

The search continued for years. For many people, D. B. Cooper became a symbol of the perfect crime. They thought he had beat the system.

Nine years passed. On February 10, 1980, eight-year-old Brian Ingram uncovered a package in the sand along the Columbia River near Portland. It contained three packs of twenty-dollar bills from the Cooper hijack money!

Was the money buried there on purpose? Did Cooper leave it to throw his pursuers off his trail? It's not likely. The edges of the bills were rounded, as if they had scraped against the river bottom. When the river was dredged in 1974, it may have brought the money to the surface and deposited it on the banks of the river.

No other clues or leads have ever been found in the D. B. Cooper case. The FBI agent originally assigned to it believes Cooper unexpectedly landed in the Columbia River when he jumped from the plane in the dark. He would have had little time to unbuckle his parachute before being dragged down by the weight of his wet clothes and the heavy bag of money.

Did Cooper drown at the bottom of the Columbia River? Is the rest of the money still in the river? Did the dredging in 1974 tear open the money bag and scatter the remaining packs of bills?

Many believe that Cooper never survived the parachute jump and that no additional trace of the hijacker or his money will ever be found. But every November 24 is D. B. Cooper Day in Ariel, Washington. Hundreds still gather to talk about the man who has become a folk hero in the Northwest. There's even a D. B. Cooper Fan Club and souvenir T-shirts!

Is Cooper long dead? Or is he alive and living a life of luxury on some South Seas island? No proof exists either way.

The Great Pyramids

"We will learn the secrets of the Great Pyramid at Giza," declared the Arab caliph Abdullah al-Mamun to the group of workers in A.D. 820. "Perhaps we will find hidden chambers filled with knowledge of the world and the stars."

"Yes, majesty," said his companions, "and perhaps we'll find great treasures beyond our imagination!"

The ninth-century caliph and his men set to work, determined to uncover the entrance to the largest of the pyramids. Unable to find the original way in, the workers cracked the limestone blocks and dug their way through one-hundred feet of rock. Their backbreaking work eventually paid off.

"At last!" shouted one of the men. "It's a narrow passageway that climbs upward. But we'll have to crawl. It's too small inside to stand upright."

The men followed the four-foot-high passage and found the original entrance to the pyramid, which had been hidden behind a stone doorway. After a careful search, they discovered another corridor, which was blocked by three huge pieces of granite.

After hours of chipping away at the limestone around the granite, the men entered a passageway that led to a twenty-foot-high room later determined to be the Queen's Chamber. It was empty.

The corridor continued, expanding to a height of twenty-eight feet with walls of polished limestone, earning it the name the Grand Gallery. Then came the largest room of all, the King's Chamber. It measured 34 feet by 17 feet by 19 feet.

Al-Mamun spotted the sarcophagus in the King's Chamber. "Look!" he exclaimed. "The actual burial coffin of the pharaoh. It's so large, the room must have been built around it."

He ordered the workers to come forward. "Bring your torches. Let's look inside." He peered into the sarcophagus. "I see nothing! It's empty! All of our work and we have found nothing!"

Did looters steal the pharaoh's remains? It's highly unlikely, since the giant granite blocks were still in place.

Why were the narrow passageways built so small that an adult found it impossible to walk upright? The Grand Gallery and other chambers were huge in comparison.

In 1951, Zakaria Goneim discovered the buried remains of an unfinished pyramid, this one six miles south of Giza. He found hundreds of pots and vessels. He also unearthed pieces of solid-gold jewelry. Entering the burial chamber, Goneim was greeted by the sight of a golden sarcophagus, still sealed after thousands of years.

After a month of careful preparation, which included taking photographs and drawing detailed diagrams, Goneim opened the stone coffin. It, too, was empty.

If pyramids were not used to bury the remains of pharaohs, then what were they used for? Few Egyptologists can agree.

The Great Pyramid of Cheops (or Khufu) takes up thirteen acres of land. Two-and-a-half million blocks of granite and limestone were used in its construction. Each block weighed many tons. It is believed that tens of thousands of workers used levers to lift, raise, and turn the stones. The huge blocks were dragged up giant ramps and transported by sleds that moved on rollers.

This pyramid is as tall as a forty-story skyscraper and dates back to about 2500 B.C. There are a total of about eighty pyramids in Egypt, all built on the Nile's West Bank. The Cheops Pyramid, along with two smaller ones at Giza, is one of the Seven Wonders of the World.

Some think the pyramids were used as astronomical observatories to chart the skies, not just as tombs or funeral monuments to the pharaohs. Several scientists believe they were used as giant

sundials to determine the seasons and length of the year.

One scientist claims that the building of the pyramids unified the tribal villages into one large work project for the good of Egypt. It gave many people something to do for the greater good of the nation.

The pyramids have been called engineering miracles. All sides are nearly identical in length, varying by only eight inches or less. The sides also line up perfectly to the points of a compass.

Egyptian knowledge of science and mathematics was not believed to be so advanced at the time of the building of the pyramids. Some feel only God could have given them such knowledge. Others say it was the work of highly intelligent beings from another world. One person even suggested that the pyramids were built by the most gifted scientists of the lost continent of Atlantis!

These incredible stone monuments have stood for almost five thousand years, and we have yet to discover all their secrets. One thing is certain, however: Long after we are gone, the pyramids will still remain.

Dorothy Forstein

January 25, 1945, was a day that Dorothy Forstein and her family would always remember. After a routine shopping trip, which included a visit to the local butcher, she returned to her Philadelphia home.

Dorothy's three children, Marcy, Merna, and Edward, were being looked after by neighbors. The sky was starting to get dark as Dorothy approached her front door and entered the large house.

Suddenly, someone ran toward her. Fists beat at Dorothy's face, and she was knocked down by something big and heavy. As she fell, the telephone was knocked over, but this didn't stop her attacker from beating her unconscious. The phone operator heard the fight and called the police.

Minutes later, the police arrived on the scene and found Dorothy lying on the floor, moaning. Her jaw and nose had been broken. Her shoulder had been fractured and she had a concussion.

No money or jewelry was taken from the Forstein home. The police assumed it was an attempted murder. But why would anyone want to kill Dorothy Forstein? She was happily married to Jules, an administrative judge in Philadelphia, and she was a devoted mother to her children.

Dorothy had no enemies. In fact, she seemed to be well liked by everyone in the neighborhood. At a loss for suspects, the police even investigated her husband. But he was working late in his office at the time of the attack.

Dorothy believed her attacker came at her from the area under the stairs. That meant he was already in the house waiting for her when she returned home. The police noted that none of the locks or windows had been broken.

How did the man get inside the Forstein house? Did he have a key? Did Dorothy interrupt him in the process of a burglary? The police found nothing missing.

Even more strange is the fact that a neighbor said she saw Dorothy return home that night and thought she saw someone with her or just behind her. Did the man come up from behind after Dorothy opened the door? Were there actually two people, or was Dorothy or her neighbor mistaken?

The police conducted a thorough investigation but never found the attacker. They assumed it was a random, senseless act of violence, and it was eventually forgotten.

But Dorothy never got over the incident. She became nervous and scared. She bought extra locks for the doors and windows and checked them constantly. Mr. Forstein hardly ever left his wife alone.

Years passed without incident. On the night of October 18, 1950, Jules had to attend a special banquet and told his wife he would be home late.

"Everything will be fine here, dear," she assured her husband. "Be sure to miss me." Jules left. Those were the last words he ever heard from his wife.

When he returned home, Dorothy was nowhere to be found, and the children were in the bedroom crying. "Mommy's gone," they wailed.

Jules couldn't believe this was happening. He thought perhaps Dorothy was visiting a neighbor or relative. He called a number of people, but no one had seen her. Dorothy's purse and keys were still at home.

The police checked all the hospitals and hotels in Philadelphia and any other place she might have gone, but they had no luck. Dorothy Forstein had completely vanished!

One of the children told the police a story so strange that at first they didn't believe it. Later, they wondered if it could be true.

Nine-year-old Marcy said that she had been awakened by a noise. She saw a man go up the stairs and into her mother's room. When the little girl walked over to Dorothy's room, she saw her mother lying facedown on the rug. The man picked Dorothy up and slung her over his shoulder.

Dorothy was silent. She was dressed in red silk pajamas and red slippers. The man, a complete stranger, wore a brown cap and jacket. He carried Dorothy down the stairs, turned the lock, and shut the door behind him. That was the last time Marcy ever saw her mother.

Nothing was missing in the Forstein house. There were no fingerprints, blood, or signs of a struggle anywhere. Psychiatrists who examined Marcy said the young girl was telling the truth.

Was the man in brown the same one who attacked Dorothy in 1945? Did he come back five years later to finish the job he started? How did he get into the house? How did he know Jules would be away that night? Did a co-worker or client of Jules' purposely harm Dorothy to get back at him?

The police found no clues, no leads, and no suspects. The disappearance of Dorothy Forstein remains an unsolved mystery to this day.

Circle of Mystery

A mysterious circle is located in Warren County, North Carolina. It is forty feet across and surrounded by a large forest.

This is no ordinary circle. It is perfectly round, almost as if special instruments were used to create it. But what makes it really unusual is that no plants or vegetation of any kind have grown within the circle for as long as people have lived in the area!

In fact, local inhabitants call it "The Devil's Tramping Ground." It is said that Satan uses this spot to walk each night. Few have had the courage to spend the night in the circle to find out.

Plants, grasses, and weeds grow to the outer edge of the circle, but not inside it. It is as if someone sprayed a very strong pesticide that made all growth within the circle die. But if that were the case, the pesticide would wear off and the vegetation would eventually come back.

Some people believe the area was the site of an old sugarcane mill. Did horses walk around the circle all day long, providing the power that ground the sugarcane into syrup? That surely would have destroyed the vegetation and could explain the circular shape. But this is not likely, since the clearing would have been overgrown by now with weeds and grass.

Another explanation is that the circle was once a place where Indian tribes gathered for special ceremonies. The result was the tramping down of all the growth. Some even believe the spot may be a secret Indian burial ground.

Soil tests performed in this mysterious circle by the state department of agriculture uncovered some interesting information. The soil was found to have no nutrients, such as organic matter and minerals, which are needed for plant growth. Yet just outside the circle the earth was perfectly normal!

What could have destroyed the nutrients in the soil? Why hasn't it absorbed the organic matter and minerals carried by wind, rain, and insects over the years?

Perfect circles don't exist normally in nature. Someone or something accidentally or deliberately made the circle.

Is it an imprint from a UFO? Did an alien spaceship land in North Carolina hundreds of years ago?

Did the materials used in the strange craft destroy the ability of the soil to ever grow anything again?

Who knows? There are no explanations. This "circle of mystery" might be a freak occurrence of nature. Or is it, as the legends say, the work of the devil?

King Arthur

Who hasn't heard about King Arthur of Britain and the Knights of the Round Table? Many people have enjoyed reading about Arthur, Merlin the Magician, Sir Lancelot, Queen Guinevere, and the sword called Excalibur.

It was a time of medieval knights and chivalry, of good and evil, of love and loyalty. But was it just a tale based on Celtic legend and mythology? Was there really a King Arthur? Did Camelot exist? Was Arthur buried on the Isle of Avalon as the story goes?

Many scholars believe the real Arthur was not a medieval knight or king, but a warrior chief of the fifth century. The British rallied around him to win a series of victories against the invading Saxons. A victory at the Battle of Badon brought peace to the land for many years.

There were only a few written historical references to Arthur. It wasn't until Geoffrey of Monmouth wrote *History of the Kings of Britain* in the twelfth century that Arthur was discussed in detail. Geoffrey referred to Arthur as the King of Britain and introduced Merlin in the story. This account became very popular, and people began to wonder whether the actual places in the story existed and where they were located.

Long ago, the area of Glastonbury in Somerset, England, was surrounded by swamps and marshland, creating an island. The Welsh called the place *Ynys Avallon*, or the Isle of Avalon. Could this be the place where Arthur was buried?

An important discovery took place on Avalon in 1191. Supposedly, the grave of King Arthur and Queen Guinevere was uncovered at the church at Glastonbury. It was said that a monk requested to be buried between the two pillars of the old church. In the course of digging, the workers discovered a lead cross seven feet down bearing the inscription "Here lies buried the renowned King Arthur, in the Isle of Avalon."

At a depth of sixteen feet, diggers discovered a hollow oak coffin. Inside were the bones of a man and a woman. Some yellow hair was discovered with the woman's remains. Legend has it that Queen Guinevere had long blond hair. The man's bones, said to be Arthur's, were very large, and the skull had a crack where a terrible blow had

been received. According to myth, Mordred, Arthur's enemy, delivered the fatal blow to Arthur. The bones were reburied in a black marble tomb, which was eventually destroyed in 1539.

There is proof that the monks at Glastonbury did uncover a grave. But was it Arthur's grave?

The lead cross, which has since disappeared, was dated as tenth century, hundreds of years *after* Arthur died. It is true, however, that the bishop at Glastonbury raised the level of the cemetery in the tenth century. Arthur's grave might have been discovered then and the lead cross placed there as a means of identification. But why didn't the bishop make Arthur's final resting place public at that time?

Many experts believe the discovery of the grave was a deliberate hoax orchestrated by the monks. Several years before, a fire destroyed most of the abbey at Glastonbury. King Henry II financed the rebuilding. His successor, Richard I, however, was more interested in financing the crusades than in rebuilding churches. Some believe the monks decided to stage a publicity stunt to raise funds for the restoration of the abbey. So they conveniently "discovered" Arthur's tomb.

Was it real or just a trick? Was Arthur actually buried at Glastonbury with Guinevere? Whose bones were in the grave? Was there really a King Arthur at all? Do people just want to believe he existed because he was so honest, noble, and good?

It's still a mystery. But the belief in the legend of King Arthur is indeed real and will probably last as long as the legends have.

Stonehenge

It was June 22, the evening of the summer solstice. The longest day and shortest night of the year marked the beginning of summer.

Thousands of people came to Stonehenge in England on this particular night. The huge stones stood silently in the darkness as they had since prehistoric times.

Many in the crowd touched the cold slabs, trying to feel their power, while others stood by quietly watching, some curious and some fearful.

Night passed, and the sky began to lighten as dawn approached. A group of druids (priests of an ancient Celtic religion) arrived, dressed in white robes. As the sun slowly rose, they performed a special ceremony in the inner area of stones.

If one stands in the middle of Stonehenge, looking out toward what is called the heel stone, one can see the sun come up over the horizon. It rises directly above the huge slab that seems to serve as a special marker to pinpoint the position of the sun. The experience is mysterious and impressive to some, yet strange and eerie to others.

What is the purpose of Stonehenge? Why was it built thousands of years ago? What special powers does it have? Scientists have been attempting to answer these questions for hundreds of years.

Located in Salisbury Plain in southern England, Stonehenge dates back to before 2000 B.C. Nearly half of the original stones are gone now, used as building materials or broken up for souvenirs.

Stonehenge consists of two types of stone arranged in an outer and an inner circle. Within the circles are horseshoe patterns of stones. At the center is a flat altar stone, which was thought to have been upright at one time but is now toppled over. Two other stones stand apart from the others. These are called the heel stone and the slaughter stone.

The outer circle and outer horseshoe pattern are made of sarsen stones originally from Marlborough Downs, twenty miles away. Each pair of these huge fourteen- to sixteen-foot stones is capped by a ten-foot slab, to resemble a doorway. The "doorways" of the outer horseshoe are nearly twenty-five feet high!

The inner circle and inner horseshoe pattern are made up of small bluestones. These come from a quarry in Wales, more than one hundred miles away.

It is believed that prehistoric peoples transported the bluestones by sea on rafts to Stonehenge. The giant sarsen stones were probably placed on rollers and sleds and hauled over land. Some estimate that it would have taken a thousand men seven years to move the sarsen stones to Stonehenge!

Most scientists agree that Stonehenge was built in four stages by a series of ancient peoples. The question is, why? Why did so many people take so much time to construct such a pattern of stones? There are many theories. Some believe that because the stones were thought to be holy, possessing special powers, Stonehenge was used as a religious site or place of worship. For many years, it was thought to have been built as a temple by the ancient druids. Others have credited the Romans for its construction.

In 1136 Geoffrey of Monmouth wrote that the magician Merlin brought the stones from Wales. Merlin used them to build a memorial to the British warriors who died fighting the invading Saxons.

In the seventeenth century, John Aubrey discovered an outer ring of fifty-six holes at Stonehenge. They had gone unnoticed because they were filled with dirt and debris. The openings became known as Aubrey Holes.

In 1965, Professor Gerald Hawkins declared that Stonehenge was built like a primitive computer, designed to predict lunar eclipses. Ancient astron-

omers tracked the movements of the moon by moving markers around the circle of Aubrey Holes.

In the late 1970s, scientist Paul Devereaux found that the Stonehenge area contained more energy currents and higher counts of radiation than other places. Some sensitive people reported the presence of psychic emissions, called memory fields. These fields allowed them to pick up visions from the past. Many UFOs have been reported over the years in the vicinity of Stonehenge.

Were the ancient peoples who built Stonehenge more intelligent and sophisticated than was ever thought possible? Or did they get help from more intelligent beings?

Was Stonehenge used as an astronomical observatory? Or was it a shrine or monument used by worshipers of the sun and the moon? What was the purpose and meaning of Stonehenge?

To this day, the secret of the mysterious slabs at Stonehenge has yet to be discovered.

Paula Welden

"I don't feel like studying right now," said eighteen-year-old Paula Welden to her roommate, Elizabeth Johnson.

The two girls were sophomores at Bennington, a small, private women's college in Vermont. It was Sunday afternoon, December 1, 1946, the end of the four-day Thanksgiving holiday. Paula had just returned from her job at the dining hall, where she waited on tables to help pay her school tuition.

Paula changed into jeans, a red parka, and white sneakers. "I'm going for a walk," she said, and went out the door.

But it's so gloomy and gray out, thought Elizabeth. "I think it's starting to rain," she said out loud, but her roommate was already gone.

Elizabeth sighed and went back to her studies.

Paula always enjoyed long walks since she had an avid interest in plants and trees.

Elizabeth Johnson never saw her roommate again!

Paula didn't return to her job that evening and still hadn't returned to her room by bedtime. The next morning, Elizabeth reported her missing.

The police found that three people had seen Paula after she left the campus that Sunday afternoon. A garage attendant on Route 67A, across from the college gates, recalled seeing a girl in red and blue run up to a nearby gravel pit, and then back again.

A man named Louis Knapp saw a girl fitting Paula's description hitchhiking on the highway. He gave her a ride to his driveway about three miles up the road. The girl had asked him questions about Vermont's famous Long Trail, a hiking path running more than two hundred miles along the Green Mountains.

The 5'5" blond student was last seen by Ernest Whitman, a night watchman for Bennington's local newspaper. She asked him for directions to the Long Trail. He was surprised to see a girl alone in the dark without hiking or snow boots.

The area was thoroughly searched by police, students, townspeople, and National Guardsmen. Rewards were posted, but no trace was ever found of Paula Welden.

Only two leads in the case were uncovered. A family who lived on the Long Trail remembered seeing a half-ton truck with New York license plates driving fast late in the evening that Paula disappeared.

Another woman recalled seeing a maroon car driving along the trail late that night. She noticed a young couple in the vehicle. One of them was a blonde woman.

Did Paula meet a young man on the trail and ask for a ride back to school? Did the truck driver offer to take her down the trail? She had already hitched a ride once that day and may have been trusting enough to take one more.

Was Paula kidnapped by either one of these drivers, or had she secretly planned to meet one of them ahead of time? Her father insisted his daughter had no serious boyfriends.

Paula did have problems. She often got depressed because she felt her father favored his two younger daughters over her. He believed college was a waste of time, and she was hurt by his lack of support for her.

Paula would often discuss her feelings with her roommate, Elizabeth. She was insecure and dissatisfied with herself. She felt she should be more independent and assertive. But these concerns weren't unusual for an eighteen-year-old girl.

It is unlikely that Paula was planning to run away or leave the area with a man. She was dressed as though she would be back soon and took no cash or ID with her.

Was Paula killed by a hit-and-run driver, or did she have a fatal accident on the trail? A thorough search did not turn up a body or any clues to her disappearance.

The year before the Paula Welden incident, a seventy-five-year-old woodsman named Middie Rivers vanished on the Long Trail without a trace. This case was unusual, as most people believed that Middie could walk the Long Trail blindfolded because he knew it so well.

Three years later, in 1949, a man named James Telford disappeared in the same area. In 1950, an eight-year-old boy vanished. Two weeks later, an experienced hiker disappeared (months later her body was found). Two more girls disappeared in 1950, both near the Long Trail.

Is it coincidence that seven people vanished between 1945 and 1950 on the eight miles of the Long Trail? Only one of the seven was ever found, and she was dead.

Some local people believe a killer was responsible. They called him the "Mad Murderer of the Long Trail," but his existence has never been proven.

Did Paula Welden run away, or was she a victim of foul play? Did she have an accident or did she meet a maniac? Can a person simply disappear from the face of the earth?

The Bermuda Triangle

It wasn't until the disappearance of Flight 19 that the world focused its attention on the strange happenings in the Bermuda Triangle.

Five torpedo bombers took off from the Naval Air Station at Fort Lauderdale, Florida, on December 5, 1945. The planes and the fourteen men aboard never came back from their mission. They vanished without a trace!

A search plane with a crew of thirteen was sent out after the missing aircraft. It, too, disappeared. In less than twenty-four hours, six planes and twenty-seven men were lost at sea. How could it have happened?

Apparently, Flight 19 leader Charles Taylor became lost. Both of his compasses went out. Radio contact faded. He became confused and drifted off course but tried to keep the formation of planes together.

"Don't come after me," he reportedly said. Instead of flying toward land, Taylor mistakenly flew farther over the Atlantic Ocean. A ship at sea reported that the rescue plane, which carried nearly two thousand gallons of fuel, exploded in midair. By the time the full-scale search was finished, not a trace of any of the planes or pilots was found.

For hundreds of years, strange incidents have been recorded in this triangular area connecting Bermuda, Florida, and Puerto Rico. Even Christopher Columbus reported problems with his compass when he sailed through this area in 1492. Columbus also described "a great flame of fire," which fell into the sea, and a strange light on the horizon.

Hundreds of ships and planes have disappeared in the Bermuda Triangle over the years. Many researchers feel that even though it is a very busy area, the number of disappearances is much too high to be normal. They believe that strange, unexplained forces may be at work.

Some think that natural phenomena, such as sudden storms, giant waves, underwater earthquakes, volcanic activity, or even waterspouts are responsible for the destruction of ships and aircraft in the area. Others feel a combination of equipment failure, bad weather, and human error can account for the strange occurrences.

Yet there are certain incidents that can't be easily

explained. On December 4, 1970, Bruce Gernon, Jr., was flying his private Beechcraft plane from Andros Island in the Bahamas to Palm Beach, Florida. He was accompanied by his father, who served as copilot.

"Look at that strange cigar-shaped cloud ahead," exclaimed Gernon to his dad. The small plane climbed to an altitude of 10,500 feet. "I can't get around it. We'll have to go through."

Once the plane was inside, the cloud seemed to rotate around the plane as if the small Beechcraft was in a tunnel. Up ahead was an opening through which Gernon could see blue sky. The plane picked up speed as it headed toward the opening, which seemed to get smaller and smaller.

As Gernon finally exited the cloud, he and his father were weightless for a few seconds. But instead of blue sky, they found themselves in a green-white haze!

"My instruments are out," he told his dad. "The compass is acting crazy and I can't make contact with radar control."

Suddenly, Miami radio crackled over the air. "How can we be over Miami Beach so soon?" Gernon thought. The haze lifted, and minutes later Gernon landed at Palm Beach.

A normal flight covers the two hundred miles from Andros Island to Palm Beach in seventy-five minutes. Gernon's flight took only forty-five minutes and covered two hundred fifty miles! After checking his gas receipts, Gernon found that he used twelve fewer gallons of gas than usual.

Did his plane fly through a time tunnel or time warp? Had it been propelled to impossible speeds that caused weightlessness? Bruce Gernon, Jr., thinks so. He believes he is one of the lucky few to feel the power of the Bermuda Triangle and live to tell about it.

Charley Ross

Every day for a week in the summer of 1874, two men in a horse and buggy deliberately rode past the Ross mansion, located in the wealthy Germantown section of Philadelphia.

The men talked to the two Ross boys, Charley, age four, and Walter, age six, and gave them chocolate and other treats during each visit. By the time the men came by on Wednesday, July 1, the boys ran to meet them as if they were old friends.

"Let's go buy some fireworks for the Fourth of July," the children suggested.

"Sounds good to me, boys," said one of the men. "Hop into the buggy and we'll go get a whole box full of sparklers and firecrackers!"

They rode eight miles into downtown Philadelphia and stopped outside a store. "Walter," said one man, "take this quarter and buy all the fireworks you want. We'll stay here and wait with Charley."

When Walter returned fifteen minutes later, the buggy was gone and so was Charley Ross!

With the help of a passing stranger, Walter came home later that evening. Hearing the story, Mr. Ross went straight to the police.

Many people in the neighborhood remembered the children riding off with the two men in the buggy. It had red-striped wheels and blue lining. But no one had seen Charley after that.

At first Mr. Ross believed his young son was simply lost in the city. It never occurred to him that this was a planned kidnapping.

After four days had passed, the worried father received a letter from the men who had taken Charley. They demanded $20,000 and threatened to kill the four-year-old.

Although the kidnappers warned him not to tell the police about their demands, Ross did, and the case was highly publicized in newspapers throughout the city. He was instructed to put the ransom money in a white bag, board a train, and throw the bag off the train when he saw a special signal.

The train was filled with police, and instead of the money, Ross put a letter in the bag. The signal never came and no contact was made. The kidnappers wrote another letter saying Ross had made a big mistake by not following their directions.

Meanwhile the kidnapping of Charley Ross was reported all across the country. It was the first publicized case of its kind, and parents suddenly took more care in watching over their children.

Through a tip, the police identified the kidnappers' letters as having been written by William Mosher, who had recently escaped from jail. His partner was a man named John Douglas, who was out of jail. But the police couldn't locate either of them.

Time passed, and another letter arrived demanding that the ransom money be handed over to a messenger at the Fifth Avenue Hotel on a certain date. Ross agreed, but no messenger ever showed up. That was the last letter sent by Charley's kidnappers.

Police continued to search for their main suspects, Mosher and Douglas, but had no luck. Then, on the night of December 14, five months after Charley was taken, two men were shot in a burglary attempt. They were identified as Mosher and Douglas. Mosher died instantly, but Douglas made a deathbed confession.

"Mosher and I stole Charley Ross," he said. "He is . . ." But before he could reveal where the boy was, Douglas died.

There are differing views as to what was said that night. One source states that Douglas said, "We killed Charley Ross." Another quotes Douglas as saying Charley would be returned safely in a few days.

Mosher's widow believed Charley was alive and her husband was going to send him home. But some feel Mosher's brother-in-law drowned the boy to get rid of him.

Was Charley still alive?

Mr. Ross never gave up searching for his son. Hundreds of people reported seeing the youngster all over the country, but all leads turned out to be false. When Ross died in 1897, his wife continued to look for Charley, never giving up hope that her son was alive.

In 1939, an aging carpenter in Arizona claimed he was the long-lost Charley, and a jury in Phoenix allowed him to use the name. When he tried to get a share of the family fortune, the other Ross children refused to accept him as their missing brother. If this man really was Charley Ross, why did he wait so long to come forward?

Did the little boy die at the hands of his kidnappers? Or did he grow up as someone else and make a full life for himself? If so, how did he escape his kidnappers?

The facts of the case will never be known.

Atlantis

Atlantis was a paradise on Earth. Fruits and vegetables grew everywhere in the rich soil. Food was plentiful. Flowers and trees covered the mountainsides. Friendly animals ran free in the forests. The wise and gentle people of Atlantis had everything they needed in their ideal, peaceful land.

But it wasn't enough. They set out to conquer the world with their great armies. The people became greedy and corrupt.

They were defeated by the Athenians. Soon after, as the story goes, "there occurred violent earthquakes and floods, and in a single day and night of rain . . . the island of Atlantis disappeared . . . and was sunk beneath the sea."

This is what the fourth-century Greek philosopher Plato tells us in two of his dialogues, *Timaeus* and *Critias*. His detailed description of Atlantis was based on information gathered by Solon, an Athenian statesman. During a trip to Egypt, Egyptian priests related the story of Atlantis to Solon, who took careful notes.

In his dialogues, Plato writes that his account of Atlantis is "wholly true," "a fact and not a fiction," and "a genuine history." But many believe that Plato's narrative was just a story invented to express his views on government, war, and the abuse of power.

According to Plato, Atlantis was a large island continent that existed around 9600 B.C. in the Atlantic Ocean. It was ruled by the ten sons of Poseidon, and Atlas was the chief king.

The main city, also called Atlantis, was circular and built around a hill. At the center of the hill was a beautiful temple and palace constructed of gold, silver, ivory, and other precious metals. Three circles of water, alternating with two circles of land, surrounded the palace. Bridges connected the land rings. Tunnels connected the water rings, through which ships could pass.

Warm and cold water fountains sprang up in the center of the city. There were elaborate baths for people and even special ones for animals. The city had many gardens and parks and even a large stadium for horse racing.

The inhabitants in the rest of Atlantis lived in

rich villages. Animals were everywhere, including herds of elephants.

But it was not enough. The people of Atlantis wanted to extend their power over others. A war with the Athenians ended in the defeat of the Atlantean armies, and soon afterward came the final destruction of Atlantis.

There are many theories about the exact location and time frame of Atlantis. Some people have devoted their lives to solving the mystery of the lost continent. In fact, nearly five thousand books have been written on the subject.

One theory states that Atlantis was the land bridge between the Old World (Europe) and the New World (the Americas) before it sank beneath the sea. Others believe the Azores, Bermuda, and the Canary islands were once the highest mountains of the continent of Atlantis.

Underwater platforms, walls, and what appeared to be buildings were discovered in the late 1960s off the coasts of Bimini and Andros islands near Bermuda. But some scientists have discounted these discoveries, saying that they were "natural" beach rock, not man-made formations from a lost continent.

Still others link the lost continent to the violent volcanic destruction of Thera, an Aegean island. Thera was once part of the Minoan civilization, which suddenly ended around 1500 B.C.

Despite these theories, there is still no concrete, indisputable evidence to support the past existence

of Atlantis. Yet people continue to search for that proof.

The lost continent of Atlantis has baffled men and women for more than 2,400 years, ever since Plato first wrote about it. Perhaps someday the mystery will be solved.

Michael Rockefeller

"These waters are unsafe," warned the missionary. "The tides along the coast are very powerful and rise to nearly twenty feet. When the tides go out," he declared, "you'll be swamped and pushed out to sea!"

"We'll be especially careful," replied Michael Rockefeller. "I've got a good boat and I'm a strong swimmer."

It was the summer of 1961. Michael was in New Guinea, a large island in the South Pacific off the coast of Australia, on a buying trip for New York's Museum of Primitive Art. He was searching for shields, painted skulls, and carved mangrove poles of the Asmat tribe, one of the native peoples of New Guinea.

A member of the wealthy Rockefeller family,

Michael was the twenty-three-year-old son of Nelson Rockefeller, who was then governor of New York. Nelson later became vice president of the United States under President Gerald Ford from 1974 to 1977.

Michael was a graduate of Harvard University and planned to attend Harvard's Graduate School of Business Administration. Before settling down, however, Michael wanted a little adventure in his life.

Along with Dr. Rene Wassink of Holland, Michael searched the coast of New Guinea for pieces of art he could send back to the museum. He and Dr. Wassink traveled in a boat made of two canoes tied together and powered by a small outboard motor.

On November 16, Michael, Dr. Wassink, and two native guides were patrolling the coastline in a swampy jungle area near the Arafura sea. Suddenly, without warning, a huge wave knocked the boat over. The two guides swam to shore for help while Michael and Dr. Wassink stayed with the boat.

With each passing hour, the boat drifted farther from shore. Michael grew impatient waiting for help to arrive. "What if nobody comes and we keep drifting out to sea?" he asked Dr. Wassink. "I think I can make it to shore."

"It's more than three miles to land," warned Wassink. "Those waters are filled with crocodiles and sharks."

"I'll use these two empty gasoline cans to keep me afloat if I get tired," declared Michael. "Don't worry, I'll make it," he said as he jumped into the water and swam away.

"I followed him until I could only see three dots, his head and the two red cans," Dr. Wassink later explained. "Then he disappeared off the horizon." It was the last time Michael Rockefeller was ever seen.

Wassink was rescued after the boat had drifted more than twenty miles out to sea. An extensive search for Michael began. Governor Rockefeller flew to New Guinea in hopes of finding his son. Helicopters, ships, and natives searched everywhere. A large reward was offered.

One gasoline can was finally found at sea more than one hundred miles away. Was it the can Michael used? If so, the chances are that he never made it to land.

Many feel he exhausted himself and drowned. Others believe he was attacked by sharks or crocodiles. Some even claim Michael Rockefeller was captured and killed by Asmat warriors.

In the thirty years since his disappearance, stories and rumors still circulate. Some claim Michael is alive but a prisoner of the Asmat tribe. Others say Michael is a spy doing undercover work in New Guinea. Another story claims Michael decided to give up his life of wealth and privilege as a Rockefeller and live with the Asmats away from the outside world.

But there is no proof to support any of these theories. Until actual evidence is found, the disappearance of Michael Rockefeller will remain a mystery.

Roanoke Island

"Look over there," the sailor said nervously, pointing.

"It's smoke coming from the settlement," shouted Governor John White, who could hardly contain his excitement.

It was 1590, three long years since White had left Roanoke Island, Virginia, six miles off the North Carolina coast. The colony was started by Sir Walter Raleigh and was supported by Queen Elizabeth. It was intended to be England's first permanent settlement in the New World.

An expedition in 1584 reported that there was plenty of food and friendly Indians on Roanoke Island. But the expedition failed to mention the stormy weather, the hard winters, and the lack of a natural harbor.

In 1585, another group traveled to Roanoke but abandoned the settlement after severe food shortages and problems with the Indians.

Raleigh didn't give up. He organized another expedition of settlers in May 1587. John White was named governor and told to settle farther north in Virginia on Chesapeake Bay. But the captain of the fleet had other ideas. He landed at Roanoke Island and refused to take the colonists any farther.

Most of the supplies were used up or lost during the difficult ocean voyage. White was asked to sail back to England to bring food and equipment for the coming winter.

England's war with Spain and a lack of financing for the settlement delayed White's return. Instead of sailing back in three months, White was forced to wait three years! Now he was anxious to see the people he left behind who were counting on him.

"These are rough waters, Governor," explained the captain. "I lost four of my men already, and the crew wants to sail on to the West Indies." The skipper smiled. "Perhaps we'll meet up with some Spanish treasure ships!"

"Please be patient, sir," replied White. "There are more than a hundred colonists on Roanoke Island. The first English child born on American soil was my own granddaughter, Virginia Dare! She was only nine days old when I left!"

After they rowed to shore, White and a group of sailors sang folk songs and blew a trumpet to announce their arrival to the colonists. But instead of a happy reunion they met with shock and disappointment.

The settlement was deserted. There were no people in sight. The smoke seen from the ship had been caused by a lightning fire.

Everything was left behind! Yet there were no signs of violence. White's books and armor were buried nearby as if they were awaiting his return.

"Over here, Governor," shouted a sailor. A tree had been stripped of its bark, and the letters *CRO* were carved on it.

"Here's another one," exclaimed the captain. This time the word *CROATOAN* was carved in large letters five feet above the ground.

White remained calm. He remembered telling the colonists to leave him a message if they decided to move to another location. "They must be at Croatoan Island," declared White. "That's about fifty miles away."

"You could be wrong, Governor," replied the captain. "Maybe they were taken prisoner by the Croatoan Indians or even massacred by them!"

"I disagree, Captain," said White. "A small cross after the message would have told me they were in trouble. But there is no cross. I'm convinced they're safe."

As preparations were made to travel to Croatoan (today called Hatteras) Island, severe storms hit the ships, and two anchors were lost. Another storm blew the vessels off course, and the captain, despite White's protests, decided to return to England.

John White never returned to search for the missing colonists. He never saw his daughter or granddaughter again. Five other search expeditions tried and failed to locate the settlers. No trace was ever found of them!

What could have happened? Did the colonists give up hope that White would return and attempt to sail to England? Were they lost at sea?

Perhaps they were taken in by the Croatoan Indians. There are Indians in North Carolina today who believe they are descendants of the Roanoke settlers. Many of these Indians have gray eyes, and some even have blue eyes and blond hair.

Others believe the settlers traveled to Chesapeake Bay, their original destination, and lived with the Chesapeake Indians. If so, they were most likely attacked and wiped out in 1607 by neighboring tribes. That same year, England's first successful permanent settlement in the New World was founded in Jamestown, Virginia.

The mystery of the fate of the Roanoke Island settlement has never been solved. It will always be known as "the lost colony."

Donald Crowhurst

A skilled sailor and navigator, Donald Crowhurst was intelligent, charming, and confident. But he was a poor businessman and never quite as successful as he had hoped to be.

Married and the father of four children, Crowhurst was an optimist who steadfastly believed a hopeless situation could always be overcome. Perhaps this was one of the reasons for his downfall.

In 1968, Crowhurst found a way to gain fame, fortune, and publicity. The *London Times* sponsored a contest open to sailors who wanted to attempt a solo trip around the world. A prize was to be awarded to the first person to complete the trip and return to England.

Crowhurst used his charm to get financial backers to build him a boat for the race. He needed something with speed and chose a trimaran. This is a boat with three hulls connected together side by side. The middle hull contains the cabin, sails, and masts, while the two outer hulls are mainly for balance. Trimarans are very fast with the wind behind them, but slow sailing into the wind.

In his mind, Crowhurst had already won the race and was entertaining thoughts of a book and movie about his experiences. He even sold the television rights to the British Broadcasting Corporation (BBC)!

The boat was called the *Teignmouth Electron* after the small English seaport. It was equipped with the latest technical gadgets, many of which weren't working properly when the race deadline arrived. But Crowhurst felt he could overcome the difficulties and still win the race. The *Teignmouth Electron* sailed on October 31, 1968.

Supplies littered the cabin. Loose wires were everywhere. Some equipment hadn't even been assembled. Crowhurst soon fell behind, sailing against the wind. Within two weeks, he had trouble with the steering mechanism and radio receiver.

He kept two separate records. On the tape recordings for the BBC, Crowhurst was always cheerful and optimistic. But in his own logbook, he wrote, "I must soon decide whether I can go on in the face of the actual situation."

After three weeks, Crowhurst came to an important decision. He would not turn back and admit defeat. Yet he couldn't continue the 'round-the-world trip either. He decided to stay in the South Atlantic area and send back radio reports as if he were still sailing around the world. When the time was right, he would sail back to England and claim the prize.

To do this, Crowhurst began writing two separate logs. One recorded what was really going on each day. The other was a fantasy log of the pretend 'round-the-world journey.

When Crowhurst radioed that he was averaging 170 miles each day, he was actually sailing only thirteen miles daily. When radio reports stated he was off the coast of South Africa or in the Indian Ocean, he was still killing time in the South Atlantic off the coast of South America. Meanwhile, he continued recording for the BBC.

As the months went by, Crowhurst began to feel guilty about what he was doing. In the real log, he wrote about his doubts and decided not to come in first place, but to settle for second place. That way, the real winner would claim the prize and Crowhurst could still get the money and publicity he desired.

By April, there was only one other boat left in the race besides the *Teignmouth Electron*. On May 21, that other boat sank, forcing Crowhurst to return and claim first prize.

As he sailed north to England to his supposed victory, his conscience began to bother him. He began to get drunk and write long, rambling, unintelligible entries in the real log. It seemed that he was slowly sinking into insanity brought on by feelings of guilt and disgrace.

Finally, on June 30, Crowhurst reported his position and cut off all radio contact. He continued writing nonsense in his real log until July 1. After that date, no other entries were recorded.

On July 11, a freighter discovered the *Teignmouth Electron* drifting in the Atlantic. No one was aboard. The ship was brought back to London, and the logs were recovered. A search began for Donald Crowhurst, but his body was never found.

Did a tormented conscience drive Crowhurst to suicide? Did he get drunk and fall overboard? Was a nervous breakdown brought on by his phony sail around the world?

Did Crowhurst prefer death over disgrace? It seems likely, but there is proof only of his disappearance, not of his death. Donald Crowhurst is "missing and presumed drowned," and his story remains one of the strangest on record.

Conquering Mount Everest

Climbing to the top of Mount Everest was the major goal in George Mallory's life. It was all he thought about, as if Everest itself had issued a personal challenge to him. Everest was the focus of Mallory's life . . . and the cause of his death.

Mount Everest is the tallest mountain in the world, rising 29,108 feet into the air. That's more than 5½ miles up, higher than many airplanes fly. Everest is located in the central Himalayas on the border between Tibet and Nepal.

Officially, Sir Edmund Hillary and Tenzing Norgay were the first men to reach the top of Mount Everest on May 29, 1953. But some believe that George Mallory was actually the first man to stand on that summit, nearly thirty years earlier.

Mallory was among the very first group to attempt to climb Everest in May and June of 1921. But snowstorms and winds of up to one hundred miles per hour thwarted their attempt.

Another expedition tried in 1922, and Mallory was among them. A sudden avalanche swept down on the climbers, and seven men plunged over the edge of a five-hundred-foot glacier cliff. One survivor said, "The others saved themselves by swimming the breaststroke in the snow."

Mallory's last attempt to climb Mount Everest took place in 1924. Six camps were set up on the mountain at various elevations. Camp Five was located at 25,000 feet, and Camp Six was established at 27,000 feet, only 2,100 feet shy of the summit.

The thirty-seven-year-old Mallory was determined to reach the top. On June 8, along with twenty-two-year-old Andrew Irvine, Mallory left Camp Six to fulfill his goal.

Irvine was an excellent athlete and an experienced mountain climber. He handled the oxygen equipment that the two men needed at such high altitudes. The thin air badly affected the reflexes and judgment of the climbers. The oxygen was needed to help keep them alert and strong.

The expedition's geologist, Noel Odell, was at Camp Five observing the summit with a strong telescope. The summit was covered in clouds. Suddenly, at 12:50 P.M., the clouds parted to reveal two moving black spots. Odell saw that the spots were Mallory and Irvine, and they were only about 800 feet from the top of Everest!

Could they reach the summit and return to

Camp Six by dark? Odell believed they were several hours behind schedule, although they seemed to be moving without any trouble. But soon, a sudden snowstorm came up and the men were lost from sight. It was the last time Mallory and Irvine were ever seen.

Odell searched for two hours with no luck. He kept shouting throughout the night and the next day in an attempt to guide the two back. Finally, on June 19, the expedition leader declared Mallory and Irvine dead. Their bodies were never found.

Many questions remain. Did the sudden storm cause the men to turn back so close to their goal? Knowing George Mallory's zeal, it is not likely.

Did one of them slip and fall? Roped together, the two climbers may have fallen to their deaths on the slopes of the mountain. Perhaps they knew they couldn't get back to camp by nightfall. Did they take shelter, fall asleep, and die from the intense cold?

And most important, did the two men reach the summit? Odell testified that they were only 800 feet from the top. Were they really the first to conquer Mount Everest, not Hillary and Norgay?

In 1933, an ax thought to belong to one of the two missing climbers was found at an altitude of about 27,000 feet. In 1979, another climber claimed to have spotted a body about 2,000 feet below the summit, but it wasn't recovered.

It is very likely that the bodies of Mallory and Irvine are still very well preserved in the high altitude of Everest, even after sixty-seven years. If

their cameras (as well as their bodies) are ever recovered, and the film can be developed, perhaps
the world would know whether these two were the
first to reach the top.

In 1924 Odell declared, "Considering the position they had reached on the mountain, I am of
the opinion that Mallory and Irvine must have
reached the summit."

Did they or didn't they? It may never be known.
Mallory once wrote, "We expect no mercy from
Everest," and he was right.

Agatha Christie

"Woman Novelist Vanishes."

"15,000 Hunt for Mrs. Christie—Result, a Blank."

"The *Daily News* offers £100 reward to the first person furnishing us with . . . information leading to the discovery of the whereabouts, if alive, of Mrs. Christie."

It was December 3, 1926. At about 9:45 that night, Agatha Christie, the famous English writer of detective novels, decided to go for a drive. She never returned home.

Was she researching one of her mystery stories? Was foul play involved?

The next morning, her green Morris motorcar was discovered abandoned off the road with the lights on and the hood up. On the seat was a coat, a small suitcase containing some clothing, and an old driver's license. But Agatha Christie was nowhere in sight!

A nearby lake was dredged for her body. Packs of dogs and light aircraft searched the countryside along with hundreds of police and thousands of volunteers. At one point, Colonel Archibald Christie, Agatha's husband, was even suspected of her murder!

Agatha was very well known, so her mysterious disappearance was followed closely in the newspapers. Ten days passed, and there were no clues as to her whereabouts. Finally, police received a tip that a woman resembling the missing writer had registered at the Harrogate Hydropathic Hotel, an elegant, expensive spa.

The woman gave her name as Teresa Neele and told guests she was from South Africa. She danced, sang, played billiards, and was very friendly. When Archibald Christie went to identify her, he saw that Teresa Neele was really his wife, Agatha.

As Colonel Christie approached his wife to speak, she didn't recognize her husband. She thought he was her brother. To the press, Colonel Christie declared, "She has suffered from the most complete loss of memory, and I do not think she knows who she is."

Several doctors supported this amnesia diagnosis. But not everyone believed that was all there was to it. To fully understand the mystery of Agatha Christie's disappearance, her personal life needs to be examined.

The year 1926 was a difficult one for Agatha. Her mother died after a long illness, and they had been very close. Her marriage was falling apart, and Agatha had recently learned that her husband was in love with another woman, whose name was Nancy Neele. In those days a divorce was hard to get, and Agatha did not want one.

Agatha was also having trouble completing her current book, *The Mystery of the Blue Train*. She was suffering from overwork and deep depression brought on by the betrayal of her husband.

Some say Agatha staged her disappearance for the publicity. This isn't likely, since she was already successful and well known. She was never comfortable with her fame and thought that publicity was vulgar.

Others say she planned her own disappearance to get back at her husband. Would she have known the police might suspect him of her murder? And why did she use the last name of her husband's lover as her own?

Agatha was a very private person. Did she expect this uproar, or did the whole incident get out of control once the press broke the story?

It is likely that a seriously depressed Agatha Christie, on the verge of a nervous breakdown, had a memory loss. Perhaps in her own distressed mind she wanted to become someone else, to escape her problems and the stress and tension of her life. Without realizing it, she took on the last name of her husband's lover, a woman she simultaneously hated and envied.

With the help of psychoanalysts, Agatha Christie was able to remember much of what happened during her mysterious disappearance. However, she was never able to recall certain missing hours, and this bothered her greatly during the course of her life.

The Christies were finally divorced in 1928. Colonel Christie married Nancy Neele and lived happily with her until his death in 1962. Agatha Christie married archaeologist Max Mallowan in 1930. They were together for forty-six years until her death on January 12, 1976.

Agatha finally finished *The Mystery of the Blue Train*, and went on to write such classics as *Murder on the Orient Express*, *Death on the Nile*, and *Witness for the Prosecution*.

In her book *An Autobiography*, Agatha never referred to her disappearance or gave any explanation for what happened. It seems fitting that the first lady of crime and detective novels never revealed the solution to her own personal mystery!

Glossary

ANNEX: to add on or incorporate one territory into another.

ANTHROPOLOGIST: a person who studies mankind, usually primitive peoples.

ARCHAEOLOGIST: a person who studies fossils and remains to learn about human life in the past.

ASSERTIVE: confident, aggressive.

AUGER: a tool used for digging holes.

CALIPH: a title used by leaders of the Islamic religion.

CHIVALRY: showing knightly qualities such as courage, nobility, and respect for women.

CRINOLINE: stiff cloth used as a lining under a skirt to make it bulge out from the waist.

DECIPHER: to make out the meaning; decode.
DREDGE: a device that is dragged along a river bottom to clean and enlarge the channel.

FLAGSTONE: a large, flat stone.

HEMP: a plant with tough fiber used to make rope.

LEVER: a bar used to move or lift things.

MAHOGANY: a type of hard wood.
MANIPULATE: to manage or control.
MISSIONARY: someone sent to another country by his or her church to teach religion.
MUFF: soft material, open at both ends, to keep the hands warm.

PARCHMENT: the skin of an animal that is specially prepared for writing on.

RANDOM: by chance or accident.
RESERVOIR: where water or any fluid is collected and stored.

SARCOPHAGUS: a stone coffin.
SHEAR: a cutting motion, as in wind shear.
STEADFAST: firm, not subject to change.

THWART: frustrate, defeat, stop.

VISOR: a mask or movable part of a helmet.

WATERSPOUT: a moving funnel-shaped column of mist and moisture that extends to the surface of a body of water.

Bibliography

Books

Baxter, John, and Thomas Atkins. *The Fire Came By*. Garden City, N.Y.: Doubleday, 1976.

Begg, Paul. *Into Thin Air*. North Pomfret, Vt.: Newton Abbot, 1967.

Berlitz, Charles. *Mysteries from Forgotten Worlds*. Garden City, N.Y.: Doubleday, 1972.

Berlitz, Charles. *Without a Trace*. Garden City, N.Y.: Doubleday, 1977.

Berlitz, Charles. *The Dragon's Triangle*. New York: Wynwood Press, 1989.

Brooksmith, Peter, ed. *The Unexplained II: Mysteries of Mind, Space, and Time.* Vols. 2 and 8. New York: Marshall Cavendish, 1985.

Christopher, Milbourne. *Houdini: The Untold Story.* New York: Thomas Y. Crowell Company, 1969.

Clapp, Jane. *Vanishing Point.* New York: The Scarecrow Press, 1961.

Cohen, Daniel. *Mysterious Places.* New York: Dodd, Mead & Company, 1969.

Cohen, Daniel. *Missing.* New York: Dodd, Mead & Company, 1979.

Downs, Robert B. *Scientific Enigmas.* Littleton, Colo.: Libraries Unlimited, 1987.

Furneaux, Rupert. *The Money Pit Mystery.* New York: Dodd, Mead & Company, 1972.

Godwin, John. *This Baffling World.* New York: Hart Publishing, 1968.

Hall, Trevor H. *New Light on Old Ghosts.* London, England: Gerald Duckworth & Co., 1965.

Harris, Reginald V. *The Oak Island Mystery.* Toronto, Canada: The Ryerson Press, 1958.

Harrison, Michael. *Fire from Heaven.* New York: Methuen, 1978.

Hayman, LeRoy. *Thirteen Who Vanished.* New York: Julian Messner, 1979.

Kraske, Robert. *Harry Houdini, Master of Magic*. New York: Scholastic, 1974.

Manguel, Alberto, and Gianni Guadalupi. *The Dictionary of Imaginary Places*. New York: Harcourt Brace Jovanovich, 1987.

Morgan, Janet. *Agatha Christie*. New York: Alfred A. Knopf, 1985.

Murray, Earl. *Ghosts of the Old West*. Chicago: Contemporary Books, 1988.

Nash, Jay Robert. *Among the Missing*. New York: Simon & Schuster, 1978.

National Geographic Society. *Mysteries of the Ancient World*. Washington, D.C.: National Geographic Society, 1979.

Nickell, Joe, with John F. Fischer. *Secrets of the Supernatural*. Buffalo, N.Y.: Prometheus Books, 1988.

O'Donnell, Elliott. *Strange Disappearances*. London, England: John Lane Ltd., 1927.

Platnick, Kenneth B. *Great Mysteries of History*. Harrisburg, Penn.: Stackpole Books, 1971.

Robyns, Gwen. *The Mystery of Agatha Christie*. Garden City, N.Y.: Doubleday, 1978.

Simon, Seymour. *Strange Mysteries from Around the World*. New York: Four Winds Press, 1980.

Spencer, John Wallace. *Limbo of the Lost*. New York: Bantam, 1975.

Time-Life Books. *Mystic Places: Mysteries of the Unknown.* Alexandria, Va.: Time-Life Books, 1987.

Tosaw, Richard T. *D. B. Cooper—Dead or Alive.* Ceres, Calif.: Tosaw Publishing, 1984.

Treharne, R. F. *The Glastonbury Legends.* London, England: The Cresset Press, 1967.

Wilson, Ian. *Undiscovered.* New York: Beech Tree Books–William Morrow, 1987.

Winer, Richard. *The Devil's Triangle 2.* New York: Bantam, 1975.

Periodicals

"At Last, the Spoor of D. B. Cooper." *Newsweek*, February 25, 1980.

"D. B. Cooper, Where are You?" *Newsweek*, December 26, 1983.

"The FBI Agent Who Has Tracked D. B. Cooper for Nine Years Retires But the Frustrating Search Goes On," *People*, March 3, 1980.

"Roanoke Lost." *American Heritage*, August/September 1985.

"Skyjacker, D. B. Cooper," *Newsweek*, November 29, 1976.

MYSTERIES OF BIZARRE ANIMALS and FREAKS OF NATURE

Earthquake!

It had been a beautiful, clear day in the Italian mountain villages near the town of Friuli. The only thing unusual was the behavior of the animals that evening.

Peasants working in the fields near the mountains of San Leopoldo heard unusual noises in the woods.

"Look there," said one villager as he pointed upward. "I've never seen anything like it in the region before."

The others glanced up to see more than a dozen roe deer huddled together on the slopes above the village. "There are more deer nearby with their heads down."

"That's strange," said another man.

"They're not grazing." He shrugged his shoulders. "Deer never come down into the valley this time of year."

The deer were not the only animals acting strangely. Chickens refused to enter their roosts. Cats in the village mysteriously disappeared. Mice and rats ran around freely. Cattle began bellowing, and the village dogs barked furiously. Many pets refused to enter the homes of their owners. At 9 P.M. on the evening of May 6, 1976, a powerful earthquake (6.5 on the Richter scale) thundered through the area. It destroyed or damaged nearly all structures. Numerous aftershocks turned what was left standing into rubble.

Did the animals sense the disaster that was to come? Do they possess a sixth sense that enables them to predict danger? Many people think so.

As early as 373 B.C., the Greek historian Diodorus wrote that all animals, especially rats, snakes, and even worms and beetles, left the town of Helice in masses one day. A few days later a violent earthquake struck, destroying the city, which sank into the Gulf of Corinth.

Throughout history, there have been accounts of the strange behavior of animals prior to earthquakes and other disasters. So many, in fact, that the Chinese have set up a nationwide earthquake alarm system by having their citizens carefully study animal behavior.

It paid off on February 4, 1975, when a 7.3 quake struck the city of Haicheng. The Chinese had predicted the disaster after noting the actions of panicked cattle, farm animals, and pets in the area. People had been evacuated into shelters. Animals and valuables had been removed from buildings. Although many structures were destroyed, few people died in the quake itself.

Some scientists believe that animals react to physical changes in the earth and the atmosphere just prior to an earthquake. Is there a rumbling or movement of the ground that animals detect before humans can? Do they notice changes in the magnetic and electrical fields of the earth's surface before an earthquake strikes? Or do animals possess extrasensory perception (ESP)—special powers beyond the normal five senses of touch, sight, hearing, smell, and taste?

Whether the explanation someday proves to be scientific or psychic, the reason for this unusual animal behavior is still a mystery. But one thing is certain. People who live around possible earthquake sites are paying closer attention to their pets and livestock. It could be a matter of life or death!

Strongheart

Before Rin Tin Tin, Lassie, and Benji, there was Strongheart, the first dog star in Hollywood. In the early days of motion pictures (during the 1920s), this magnificent-looking German shepherd was the top-ranked movie star and the biggest box office attraction in the world.

In a personal appearance tour across the country, Strongheart's train was met by thousands of admirers, both young and old, from coast to coast. He was awarded keys to the cities he visited, and he always stayed in the best hotel suites.

Strongheart came to America from Germany, where he was a champion police and war dog. He weighed about 120 pounds and was powerfully built. But it was his face that revealed a unique intelligence and understanding.

Allen Boone wrote about his relationship with this extraordinary dog in his book *Kinship With All Life*. Strongheart was often sent toys, which were all kept in one particular closet, by his admirers. When he felt like playing with a toy, the dog would open the closet door with his mouth, pick out one toy he liked, back out of the closet, close the door behind him, and take the toy outside.

When Strongheart was finished playing, he would bring the toy back, open the closet door, replace the toy, back out, and close the door. He did these things on his own, without a trainer guiding him, without treats, and without hand signals!

If Strongheart wanted to go outside, he opened the door himself and went out. When it was time for bed, he barked and pulled Boone into the bedroom. When it was time to get up, he barked again and tugged at Boone's pajamas. He was a superstar and used to having his own way.

One incident in particular made Boone realize how remarkable Strongheart really was. Boone was working at his typewriter on a beautiful spring morning. He began thinking about how nice it would be to stop everything and take Strongheart into the hills for a long walk.

Boone hadn't even gotten out of his chair when the back door crashed open and Strongheart ran excitedly into the room. He licked Boone's hand, rushed into the bedroom, and came out with the old sweater Boone wore whenever they went outside. After dropping the sweater at Boone's feet, Strongheart ran back to the bedroom and came back with Boone's jeans. After three more trips to the bedroom, Strongheart had brought everything they would need for their outing together.

How did Strongheart know Boone had decided they would go for a walk? There was only one way. Strongheart had read Boone's mind! In fact, he had probably been reading his mind all along, but Boone never noticed. Some people might say the dog interpreted the man's movements and gestures and concluded they were going outside. But Strongheart wasn't even in the room at the time!

Boone spent much of his time trying to establish a two-way form of telepathic communication with the animal. After a while, Boone and the dog became inseparable, and the two learned to share a special psychic connection.

There's no doubt that Strongheart was a remarkably intelligent creature who possessed powers far beyond those of the average dog. But did Strongheart have extrasensory perception? Allen Boone believed without a doubt that he did.

Killer Bees

Fifteen hundred people waited patiently on the international bridge connecting the cities of Uruguaiana, Brazil, and Passo de los Libres, Argentina. Farmers were taking their fresh fruit to market, and tourists were traveling from one country to another.

"What's taking so long?" complained one man.

"Calm down," said his companion. "It takes time for the customs agents to check everyone's papers and inspect the cargo."

"What time is it anyway? The smell of the fruit is making me hungry."

"It's ten A.M. We'll grab a bite to eat when we get off the bridge."

"What is that high-pitched noise?" a nearby woman asked. "It sounds like buzzing to me."

Before anyone could react, the air was thick with angry flying insects. A huge swarm of thousands of African bees, attracted by the fresh fruit, attacked the people on the bridge. Within seconds, the buzzing of the bees was drowned out by screams and cries of pain and terror.

The people panicked. Some ran off the bridge trying to protect their face and head from the onslaught of stings. Others jumped off the bridge into the river below.

Those who were sensitive to insect bites went into shock from the venom of multiple stings. The bees covered the fruit trucks so thoroughly they didn't look like trucks anymore.

Fire departments from both cities fought the bees for hours. When the dust had settled, it looked like a major war zone. More than one thousand people had to be hospitalized, some in serious condition. One man had been stung sixty times in the face and head.

This wasn't a scene from a television movie of the week. It really happened on December 5, 1975. The question is, how did normally gentle, productive honeybees turn into these fierce and vicious creatures?

It all began in 1957. A geneticist named Warwick Kerr was conducting bee-breeding research experiments at the University of São Paulo in Brazil. Kerr wanted to increase the honey production of the Brazilian bees, which were the gentle, European type.

Kerr decided to crossbreed African queen bees with the European variety. The African type was known for its aggressive behavior and high rate of honey production. Kerr's plan was to breed a gentle, but more productive, honeybee.

Disaster struck. Twenty-six African queens were accidentally released from their hives and quickly established new colonies in the nearby forests. They began to crossbreed with the local bees, resulting in a new strain of fierce African bees. The local bees were overwhelmed and the African bees spread throughout the country and parts of South America.

The slightest disturbance causes the African bees to release alarm pheromones that act as an attack signal to the swarm. The bees react so quickly that people or animals are unable to defend themselves and may die of massive stinging.

Killer bees have been responsible for hundreds of deaths across Central and South America. For every death, thousands more have been hospitalized. The bees continue to travel northward into Mexico and the United States.

The first confirmed attack by killer bees in the United States took place on June 5, 1991, in Brownsville, Texas. A maintenance man unknowingly ran over a hive with a power lawn mower. He was stung eighteen times but survived the attack.

Once thought to be better honey producers, the African bees are now known to be responsible for a 60 to 70 percent drop in honey production in Central and South America. U.S. farmers are worried how this might affect American honey production as well as the pollination of fruit and vegetable crops that are also dependent upon bees.

Scientists are attempting to unlock the mystery of the African honeybee. They hope to find a way to allow the European bee to take back its position of dominance. In the meantime, the killer bees are here to stay.

Late, Great Dinos

The giant ten-ton dinosaur, sensing danger, lifted its enormous head to scan the horizon. Suddenly a flash of light, one hundred times brighter than the sun, filled the sky. In an instant, the largest and most ferocious creature that ever lived was burned to a cinder.

Was this how Tyrannosaurus Rex and other prehistoric beasts suddenly became extinct 65 million years ago? Some people think so.

According to Michael Allaby and James Lovelock, authors of *The Great Extinction*, an enormous object from space, weighing more than 100 billion tons and traveling twenty times faster than a rifle bullet, which moves at about 2,800 feet per second, crashed into the north Atlantic Ocean. This collision with Earth would have caused an explosion 5 billion times stronger than either of the atomic bombs dropped on Japan in 1945!

Huge amounts of water and debris would have violently shot into the atmosphere, polluting the air and blocking the sun. Darkness, flooding, earthquakes, and tidal waves throughout the world would have been the result of such an impact.

The small percentage of creatures that lived through the catastrophe would have had to exist in a darkened environment with little remaining vegetation. Few of the large animals could have survived, but many small mammals would have lived on, eating seeds, spores, and what remained of the plant life.

It might have happened this way, but no one knows for sure. Scientists disagree as to whether the dinosaurs died out quickly, as described above, or whether the process was a gradual one lasting thousands or even millions of years.

Dr. Robert T. Bakker, author of *The Dinosaur Heresies*, believes the extinction occurred gradually. The shallow seas that

covered large land areas during the Age of the Dinosaurs began to drain away from the continents. Land bridges emerged, allowing different species to travel to other parts of the world. Each species brought with it foreign parasites and bacteria. This species exchange might have unleashed new diseases among the dinosaurs from which they never recovered.

Bakker believes a meteorite or large asteroid might have struck the Earth long ago, but it killed off only the few surviving dinosaurs. The main cause of the dinosaur's disappearance was widespread unchecked disease, similar to the bubonic plague that swept through Europe in the fourteenth century.

Other extinction theories range from changes in climate to starvation to overcrowding. According to Dr. Tony Swain, an English botanist, chemist and author of numerous books including *Plants in the Development of Modern Science*, the large plant-eating dinosaurs (herbivores) ate huge quantities of flowering plants that contained large amounts of alkaloids. Did the plant-eaters die of alkaloid poisoning? If the answer is yes, then the flesh-eaters (carnivores) died soon after, since they depended on the plant-eaters for their own existence.

As time goes on, new pieces of the puzzle surrounding the death and disappearance of the dinosaurs will be uncovered. But there are still many unanswered questions. Will the riddle ever be completely solved? Until it is, it will remain one of the great mysteries.

The Snake That Took Revenge

Do animals feel the same kind of emotions that people do? There are numerous stories of grief suffered by animals when they lose a mate, an owner, or even a friend. It follows that if they feel grief, they could feel other emotions too, such as joy, depression, satisfaction, and even revenge.

Can animals feel revenge, an emotion that requires reason, thought, and action? An interesting true story about a snake's revenge was described in a book by Alexander Key called *The Strange White Doves*.

Key's uncle lived in Florida when he was a young man. One day he was clearing some of the land around his house so he could plant a garden. While he was trying to dig up an old tree stump, it broke open, revealing a pair of small brown snakes.

Key's uncle was surprised and frightened. When he saw markings on the snakes similar to a rattler's, he reacted without thinking. He swung his pickax and tried to kill the creatures.

Had the man taken a few seconds to think, he would have realized that they were harmless king snakes that killed mice and other rodents. They were more valuable to him alive than dead. But it was too late. The pickax came down like a guillotine, killing one snake instantly. The other escaped. From that day on, it began to stalk Key's uncle to take revenge for the murder of its companion.

Although the man was sorry for killing the snake, he wasn't very upset at first, even when he noticed the surviving snake start to follow him whenever he left the house. He didn't think the creature would continue this behavior for very long, but he was wrong. The king snake turned up everywhere and began to make Key's uncle very nervous.

When he was working outside near the house, the man would turn suddenly and see the snake only a few yards away. He was sure it was watching him carefully, waiting for an opportunity to strike.

The man would sit on the porch of his house and watch the snake slither up to the windows and screen door. He knew it was searching for a way to get into the house.

This went on for weeks and weeks. According to Key: "He had destroyed its home and killed its mate, and it sought revenge with the only weapon it had that might succeed against a man."

Key's uncle was in such a state of panic that he felt he had to kill the snake to preserve his sanity. He hid weapons for this purpose all over the grounds, in case the snake surprised him. The small creature continued to outsmart the man, until one fateful day the snake slithered too close and Key's uncle grabbed a hoe and killed it.

The man was haunted by the incident throughout his life. So, in a strange way, the snake did get its revenge.

Wanted:
A Living Coelacanth

It was a routine fishing trip along the coast of southern Africa for the trawler *Nerine* on December 22, 1938. Little did Captain Hendrik Goosen and his crew know that they would soon be involved in one of the most important discoveries of the twentieth century.

The trawler dragged large nets along the bottom of the Indian Ocean, trapping many different kinds of fish that were later sold. If Goosen found anything interesting or unusual in his nets, he would notify Marjorie Courteney-Latimer, curator of the East London Natural History Museum. She collected specimens for the museum and hoped to identify new or unusual species.

By the time the *Nerine* docked at New London that morning, the day was already hot and bright. Along with the usual number of small sharks, rat tails, rays, and other assorted creatures, Goosen noticed a large fish at the bottom of the pile. It was about five feet long and dark blue in color with big blue eyes. What was really unusual was its odd-looking fins that resembled legs.

Goosen notified Courteney-Latimer, who admitted she had never seen anything like it before. She took it to the museum and examined the fish closely. It was fifty-four inches long and weighed 127 pounds. The fish's blue color had changed to gray-black, and its whole body was covered with sharp, bony scales.

Courteney-Latimer quickly sent a letter and a sketch of the fish to Professor James L. B. Smith at Rhodes University, 350 miles away. She hoped he would be able to identify what she thought was a very primitive creature. By the time Smith's reply was received, the fish had been mounted to prevent total decay and its internal organs had been thrown away.

Smith believed Courteney-Latimer had made an incredible discovery. It looked very

much like a fossil fish called a coelacanth (pronounced "SEAL-uh-canth"). However, the last fish of this type had supposedly become extinct with the dinosaurs millions of years ago!

Seven weeks after the fish had been pulled from the Indian Ocean, Professor Smith finally arrived in East London to see the mounted specimen. "That first sight hit me like a white-hot blast . . ." he said. "It was true, it really was true. It was unquestionably a coelacanth."

Why all this excitement about a fish? Here was a creature that was thought to have existed 300 million years ago and was considered extinct. This fish had been identified previously only by its fossil remains, and the discovery of a living specimen was proof that the coelacanth was alive today in the twentieth century!

Smith was sure there must be other living coelacanths, and he was determined to find them. He printed and distributed posters in South African ports offering a reward for two more specimens.

Smith had no idea that it would take fourteen years for a second coelacanth to be discovered. In December of 1952, a fisherman named Ahmed Hussein caught the fish near one of the Comores Islands off the coast of

Mozambique. Although it was slightly damaged, the fish contained many of its internal organs.

A third specimen was caught in 1953, also near the Comores Islands, now thought to be the central home of the coelacanths. At this time, the French government took control of the project since the islands were French territory. Over the years dozens of specimens were caught, studied, and even presented to museums throughout the world for exhibit.

It wasn't until 1987 that underwater film was taken of live coelacanths swimming in their own environment. The next big challenge for scientists is to capture a living fish and keep it alive for observation.

The discovery of the coelacanth is an example of cryptozoology, the study of and search for hidden and as yet unidentified living animals. The coelacanth, thought to be extinct 70 to 80 million years ago, was discovered by chance. What other mysterious creatures are waiting to be detected in the depths of the sea or other unexplored regions of the world? Time will tell.

Lady Wonder

Lady Wonder read people's minds and located lost valuables. She correctly predicted the outcome of elections and sporting events. What was especially amazing was that Lady Wonder was only a year old when she began to exhibit these special talents!

She became famous in the late 1920s for her psychic ability. For nearly thirty years Lady Wonder was the subject of many newspaper and magazine articles. She couldn't speak very well so she used a typewriter to communicate with others.

In case you haven't guessed, Lady Wonder was a horse—an incredible black-and-white filly. Owned by Mrs. Claudia Fonda of Richmond, Virginia, Lady Wonder first made headlines in 1928 with her ability to solve arithmetic problems.

Mrs. Fonda developed a special typewriter for the horse to use, with extra large keys made of soft rubber that could be easily operated. The typewriter had the alphabet and the numbers zero through nine on the keys. The horse touched her muzzle to the proper key and a number or letter would flip up. In this way, Lady Wonder could talk to anyone.

In a 1932 interview with a reporter from a Richmond newspaper, Lady was asked who would be nominated by the Democratic party for president of the United States. The horse typed "ROO," then stopped, looked around, and typed out "I can't spell the name." The Democratic presidential candidate turned out to be Franklin Roosevelt, who was elected president four straight times, in 1932, 1936, 1940, and 1944.

The reporter thought that Mrs. Fonda could have given special signals or made gestures to Lady Wonder to tell her how to respond. So the reporter then asked the horse to type out her middle name, which was not known to Mrs. Fonda. The horse responded correctly and also typed out numbers the reporter and her assistant had written on hidden pieces of paper.

Many people questioned Lady Wonder's abilities until she touched them directly. Author Morey Bernstein, who wrote about reincarnation in *The Search for Bridey Murphy*, lost his luggage on a plane trip from Denver, Colorado, to Houston, Texas. The airline couldn't locate the bags, which contained important papers and information. Bernstein consulted Lady Wonder, who said the luggage was sitting in a New York airport. Much to the embarrassment of the airline, that's exactly where it turned out to be.

When Lady Wonder regularly predicted the results of horse races, racing officials put a stop to it. She even helped the police find missing children successfully.

Over the years, this amazing horse was an object of study by doctors, professors, and psychologists. They often insisted that Lady's owner leave the testing area so the horse wouldn't be influenced in her responses by any gestures or bodily movements. Then a screen was placed between Lady and her questioners so she wouldn't respond to gestures unknowingly made by them. The horse provided answers so quickly and correctly that Dr. J. B. Rhine of Duke University concluded that Lady Wonder read their thoughts using extrasensory perception (ESP).

Did the horse get the correct answers and make predictions by reading other people's minds? Is it possible that Lady Wonder used her own intelligence and reasoning processes to come up with the correct answers and predictions?

In the case of Morey Bernstein's luggage, no one knew where the bags were, so telepathy wouldn't have helped the horse locate them. Apparently, Lady was clairvoyant— able to locate missing objects or people by using special abilities beyond the normal five senses. By correctly predicting the outcomes of elections and sporting events, Lady Wonder showed that she also had the power of precognition—knowledge of events before they actually happen.

For nearly three decades, this amazing horse performed remarkable feats that could be explained only in terms of ESP and other paranormal phenomena. After a long and successful career, Lady Wonder had a heart attack and died on March 19, 1957.

King

The Carlsons rescued King one snowy Christmas Eve in 1975. The half German shepherd, half husky pup had apparently been abandoned by his owner. He had been left for dead with a bullet wound in his head. Nursed back to health by the Carlsons, the dog became "king" of the Carlson farm in Granite Falls, Washington.

Five years later, at Christmastime, a fire broke out in the Carlsons' kitchen at about 3:30 in the morning. Everyone was sound asleep. Suddenly, King ran into seventeen-year-old Pearl Carlson's bedroom, grabbed hold of her arm, and pulled her out of bed. Awake now, Pearl saw the thick black smoke spreading through the house. "Fire!" she screamed. "The house is on fire!"

Fern Carlson woke up quickly and led her ill husband, Howard, to the bedroom window of their one-story house. "Jump outside," she said. Then Fern went to find her daughter and guided her to a window. They both escaped.

Hearing a whining sound coming from the burning house, Fern realized King was still inside. "Come, King," she commanded the dog. But instead of jumping outside, the animal ran deeper into the house.

Immediately, Fern understood King's strange behavior. Her husband must still be inside! Fern climbed back through the window into the house, and King led her to Howard, who had collapsed on the floor. With great difficulty, Fern managed to break open a window, and she and Howard jumped to safety. King refused to move until all of the Carlsons were safe.

The house burned to the ground, but everyone was okay. King's hair was scorched by the fire, and the pads of his feet were burned and swollen. His metal collar had become so hot from the flames that it seared the flesh around the dog's neck.

King saved the lives of the Carlsons that night, but no one knew how he had gotten into the house to warn Pearl. He slept in the recreation room off the kitchen, but the door into the house had been closed.

When King refused to eat after the fire, the Carlsons discovered that he had long, painful wood splinters in his mouth and jaw. To save his beloved family, King had frantically chewed through the wooden kitchen door to get into the house to sound the alarm. It's no wonder that King was named the Ken-L Ration Dog Hero of the Year in 1981!

What powers of intelligence, reasoning, and loyalty did this animal possess to risk his own life to save others? When the way into the house was blocked, the dog could have easily escaped through the pet door into the backyard. Yet he chose to chew through the kitchen door, enduring much pain, to get into the house.

Was it merely instinct that governed the actions of King and led him to save his family? Or was it something more, a mystery that cannot be explained within the normal understanding of the abilities of animals?

Bloodsuckers

It was a warm summer night. The young woman tossed and turned restlessly in her sleep. The second-floor balcony doors had been left open to let in the night air.

Scattered clouds covered the face of the full moon. A slight breeze ruffled the window drapery. Only the sounds of hooting owls and other nocturnal creatures could be heard.

Suddenly, a large, black-winged bat flew through the open balcony doors and circled above the bed of the sleeping woman. The clock chimed midnight as the bat changed into a human male figure dressed entirely in black. As he bent over the sleeping form, the man pulled back his lips to reveal large canine-type fangs.

As the fangs of the dreaded vampire pierced the throat of the young woman, she moaned aloud, but she did not awaken. The creature feasted on the woman's blood. When the vampire was satisfied, it changed back into a bat and flew out into the night.

The young victim awoke the next morning feeling even more tired than when she went to sleep. She looked pale and unhealthy and wondered to herself, "What are those two small marks on my neck?"

This is a typical scene from one of those old late-night vampire movies starring Bela Lugosi. But everyone knows there are no such things as vampires—or are there? Except for the part where the bat turns into a man and then back into a bat again, this scene could have really happened! Vampire bats do exist and have been known to drink the blood of unsuspecting people!

There are nearly one thousand species of bats, but only three live exclusively on blood. In fact, their throats are too small to swallow anything else. Two bat species feed on the blood of birds, but the third feasts on cattle, horses, and sometimes even humans!

The small, brown vampire bat has a mouth full of razor-sharp teeth. It uses its

two upper center teeth (called incisors) to puncture the skin. Instead of sucking the blood, as vampires supposedly do, the vampire bat laps it up with its tongue from the wound of its unfortunate victim.

A chemical in the bat's saliva contains an anticoagulant that allows the blood to keep flowing by not allowing it to clot. The vampire bat will feed for twenty to twenty-five minutes before it is full. Strangely enough, its victims are unaware they have been bitten by these creatures, although loss of blood can cause weakness and lower resistance to disease.

The main danger in the bite of a vampire bat is that it may carry rabies, a disease that can be deadly to people and other animals. Vampire bats are found in South and Central America. They sleep during the day and feed only at night.

Nearly all legends have some basis in fact. It's not a coincidence that vampire stories and bats are connected with one another. One need only learn a little about the very real and unusual vampire bat to discover one of the strangest mysteries of nature.

The Killer Sea Wasp

It was a beautiful day to be at the beach. The sun was shining, and the sky was bright blue and cloudless. The water was warm and clear.

Thousands of sunbathers flocked to the beaches near North Queensland, Australia, to relax, get some color in their cheeks, and have fun. Families spread blankets on the sand and distributed food and drink to adults and children.

The toddlers and younger children, under the watchful gaze of parents, played in the wet sand near the water. The older children waded into the shallows.

An eleven-year-old girl waved to her

mother, who was sitting on a blanket. The girl was about fifty feet from shore, in water that barely reached her knees. The girl never saw the colorless, bell-shaped body of the jellyfish as her legs brushed against it in the water. Had she seen this particular species, called the sea wasp, she might have thought it to be quite beautiful and fragile-looking.

From the exact moment the girl's legs touched the trailing tentacles of the jellyfish, all she was aware of was a terrible burning pain. Then she collapsed into unconsciousness. By the time other bathers carried the girl to shore, she was dead, a victim of one of the most deadly creatures on earth.

An autopsy of the girl's body revealed that her lungs and respiratory system were congested and filled with mucus. Marks on her legs showed numerous tentacle stings.

Some people believe this girl was one of the lucky ones. Unconsciousness and death in less than a minute are preferable to the usual symptoms of sea wasp victims. These symptoms include agonizing pain, blindness, muscle spasms, sweating, and shortness of breath for minutes and possibly hours before eventual heart failure and death.

If the unfortunate victim is stung in deeper water, he or she may drown before

getting to shore. It is believed that many drowning deaths in northern Australia are actually the result of sea wasp stings.

The body of the sea wasp ranges from about two to eight inches across and is four to five inches wide. It's made up mostly of water and is clear in color. As many as fifty tentacles trail away from the corners of the body, sometimes reaching lengths of up to four feet.

Each tentacle has thousands of tiny stinging cells called nematocysts. Each nematocyst injects venom into the unfortunate victim like a doctor injects medicine in a hypodermic needle into a patient's arm.

The sea wasp uses its tentacles to locate food and as a self-defense mechanism. They're often found in shallow water close to shore, searching for bottom-dwelling shrimp to eat. Sea wasps live in the waters around Australia, the Bahamas, Brazil, the Philippines, and even the south Atlantic coast of the United States.

The venom of this deadly creature is believed to be the strongest, most potent that exists in nature. It's no wonder that sea wasps are more feared than sharks or cobras! Although other jellyfish stings are treatable, there is no way to counteract the venom of the sea wasp.

Until scientists solve the problem of discovering an antidote, the sea wasp will continue to threaten beach lovers and swimmers with its painful sting of death. The fact is, even if an antidote is someday found, there may not be enough time to use it!

Sam's Journey

When Debbie and Ray Foltz moved from Montrose, Colorado, to Santee, California, in 1983, they had to make an important decision. They couldn't take both their dogs with them.

With two pets, Debbie and Ray were afraid nobody would rent them a home. They decided to leave Sam, their one-year-old Yorkshire terrier–poodle mix, with a friend in Montrose. Sam's mother, the other dog, traveled to California with the Foltz family.

Sam missed his family so much that one night he left his new home in Montrose and began an amazing journey. The little dog traveled on foot through four states and across 840 miles. No one knows how he did it, but one day a dirty, exhausted, and hungry Sam turned up outside the door of the new Foltz home in Santee!

Debbie and Ray could hardly believe it was the dog they had left behind. "Walking here is the only way he could have made it," said Debbie. "His paws were all worn and hurt. He was suffering from malnutrition and muscle spasms when he showed up at our door."

Right away, Sam's mother went to work licking and cleaning her son. Debbie and Ray took the little dog to the veterinarian, who tended to his wounds. Sam was his old self in a few days.

"I don't know how he managed to find us. It's just one of those miracles you hear about," explained Debbie.

What makes Sam's journey so incredible is not the fact that the dog was so small and the distance so far. Rather, it was the fact that Sam had no idea where the family was headed. How could he have known where they were moving? How could he have known which direction to travel?

The tiny terrier walked out of Colorado, possibly into Utah or New Mexico, through Arizona, the Mojave Desert, and then to Santee in Southern California. Finally, he managed to locate the exact house of the Foltz family. How did he do it? How did Sam seek out and find his owners?

Scientists don't really know how dogs can travel through strange cities, over highways, and even across mountains and rivers they have never seen before. Some call it "the homing instinct," although there's no proof that it is an instinct. Others say it's a type of extrasensory perception called psi-trailing or "orientation by unexplained means."

There is no way to know how Sam endured the physical part of the journey in addition to following the trail of the Foltz family. Did the terrier share a psychic bond with Debbie and Ray? Did he read their minds, following their route and location?

Science cannot explain this phenomenon, and the mystery remains unsolved.

The Archerfish

The leafy plants that hang over the banks of the small streams in Southeast Asia are populated with many insects and spiders. Inches above the surface of the water, the small creatures are unaware that they are being stalked.

The danger comes from the water below. A fish swims near the surface of the stream, then stops directly below a small spider resting on some vegetation. The spider is more than six inches above the fish, whose eyes seem to focus directly on the small creature.

The fish's mouth breaks the surface, opens slightly, and suddenly spits several drops of water directly at the spider. The insect is hit, falls into the stream, and is immediately eaten by the fish, called the archerfish.

The unusual archerfish has the unique ability to shoot down insects above the surface of the water. It grows up to twelve inches in length and is found mainly in waters of the South Pacific and Southeast Asia.

Although much of its food consists of shrimp, insect larvae, and other small water creatures, the archerfish prefers to eat the live food it stalks and shoots. Occasionally it can bring down flying insects, not just those at rest.

The shape of the fish's mouth gives it the ability to shoot a stream of water as a weapon. There is a groove in the roof of the mouth that, when the tongue presses upward against the groove, forms a narrow tube. The water is then driven through the tube when the gill covers are closed.

An adult archerfish can accurately hit insects with a stream of water up to six feet or more above the surface! On the rare occasion when the fish misses its mark, the aim is adjusted and other shots quickly follow.

The force of the water spit by an archerfish can knock an insect high in the air. People who have been hit by the stream have said the water stung their face.

The mystery of the archerfish revolves

around the question of intelligence. Some believe its eyes are more advanced than other fish, allowing them to focus and judge distance accurately. Others point to the fact that their aim can be adjusted and improved, showing that it's more of a learned ability.

An example of this type of ability took place in an aquarium exhibit of 150 archerfish in a large tank. According to Maurice and Robert Burton, in the *Encyclopedia of Fish*, at feeding time the water level was lowered and small bits of hamburger meat were thrown against the sides of the tank above the surface of the water. The fish started to spit water at the meat. Within minutes, much of the hamburger washed down from the sides of the tank into the mouths of the hungry archerfish.

In *Strangest Creatures on Earth*, Edward M. Weyer, Jr., wrote about a friend in Thailand who entertained guests with special performances of archerfish. His balcony was directly over the water, and the fish would congregate each day and wait for small food scraps to be thrown to them. When a spider or cricket was tied by a thread to a pole and lowered to several feet above the water, the archerfish exhibited their shooting skills as they tried to catch their meal.

Weyer noted that on two separate occasions the fish put out his friend's cigarette while he sat reading a newspaper!

Is it instinct that causes the archerfish to shoot accurately at its targets, or is it intelligence that directs its actions? Scientists don't know.

The "Bomber" Beetle

The bird was gathering insects to feed her young when it spotted the ground beetle under a rock. The beetle's body was a bright orange-tan color with blue-black wing covers. It was small and looked harmless, and the bird thought it might be a tasty treat.

As the bird bent to pick up the insect, there was a loud popping sound. A foul-smelling stinging fluid spurted out of the beetle, hitting the bird right in the face. It squawked in pain and surprise and dropped the beetle instantly. The bird's eyes were burning as it flew quickly away. Never again would it bother another bombardier beetle!

Just as the bombardier on military aircraft dropped bombs of destruction on war-time targets, the bombardier beetle shoots bombs of burning chemicals on its enemies. Whenever it is attacked or threatened, the beetle's rear end turns into a cannon, firing up to twenty-nine shots in succession before resting and refueling if necessary.

Scientists have found that the mixture of chemicals that make up these "beetle bombs" is boiling hot and can cause an angry red welt on human skin.

The firepower of the bombardier beetle comes from two glands in its abdomen. Several chemicals are stored within the glands. When mixed together, they create a powerful reaction that causes the compound to shoot from the beetle's body. This mixture has been described as a "hot, stinging spray."

The bombardier beetle is just one of nearly 250,000 species of beetles, ranging in size from a hundredth of an inch to more than eight inches in length. The beetles' tough, hard outer bodies are so strong, they can carry loads one thousand times their own weight!

There are endless varieties of beetles. One type eats the lead covering on telephone cables, while another eats grain. Still others bury small dead animals underground to eat at a later date. The most popular and useful

of beetles are ladybugs, which help farmers by eating aphids and other insects that attack fruit crops.

Bombardier beetles are half an inch long and live mainly in tropical and subtropical climates throughout the world. They are common carnivorous (meat-eating) beetles, and they rest during the day and hunt for food during the night.

The mystery of the bombardier beetle isn't the unique method of self-defense it uses against enemies, including large ants, reptiles, and birds. Rather, the mystery is how this small insect can store and use such acidic chemicals without being burned or injured.

Scientists think that the secret lies in the beetle's hard outer skeleton of armor, called the chitin, which seems to be used especially for this protective purpose. Until the answer is clear, scientists will continue to study this problem. The bombardier's body is unique in that it can store and use acidic chemicals without injury. The question is, how?

Giants of the Deep

The octopus has a bad reputation. Many people believe it's a giant long-armed monster that lives in the depths of the ocean. It eagerly waits to kill divers and drag ships to a watery grave. That's how author Jules Verne described the creature that attacked the submarine *Nautilus* in *20,000 Leagues Under the Sea*.

Incidents like the one described above are likely to apply to the giant squid, which is more aggressive than the usually timid octopus. A squid will attack prey with its ten long arms and then tear it apart with its sharp and powerful beak. One giant squid measured fifty-seven feet, including thirty-five-foot-long tentacles!

The squid's main enemy is the sperm whale. At about sixty feet long, it's one of the largest creatures in the world. The two often battle to the death. Large tentacle marks on the bodies of captured sperm whales indicate they were attacked by giant squids at least two hundred feet long! Although a squid of this size has never actually been seen by man, it is believed to exist in the unexplored depths of the ocean.

In contrast to the squid, an octopus is a loner by nature and will generally avoid confrontation. It has eight, not ten, tentacles and changes color to blend into its surroundings when threatened or afraid. It can stretch and flatten itself to slip through the smallest of spaces. Some large octopuses measure thirty feet across, including tentacles, and most are very shy. They move slowly over the ocean's bottom, while the squid moves quickly through the water pursuing its prey.

Scientists have admitted the existence of the giant squid, but they are hesitant about supporting the existence of a species of giant octopuses, even though one specimen has already been identified.

It all started one day in November of 1896, nearly one hundred years ago. Two boys were bicycling on Anastasia Beach near Saint Augustine, Florida. Quite by accident they came upon what was later called "The Florida Monster."

They parked their bikes to investigate a huge carcass half buried in the sand. When they saw its enormous size, the two boys quickly went for help, and Dr. DeWitt Webb of Saint Augustine was called in. He concluded that the body was that of a large whale that had washed up on the beach. After closer examination, armlike extensions thirty-two feet long were found under the sand. The main body of the creature was twenty-three feet long and eighteen feet wide.

Webb believed he had found the body of a giant octopus and notified Professor Verrill of Yale University. In the meantime, he cut and preserved tissue samples from the specimen.

Without seeing the carcass, Verrill first decided it was a squid. After looking over photographs and other information, he changed his mind and said it was an octopus. Then, after examining tissue samples, he finally concluded the creature was a whale after all. At no time did Verrill ever examine the actual remains of the creature.

Many years passed. In 1957, Forrest Wood, a marine biologist, became interested in "The Florida Monster." Wood discovered that the Smithsonian Institution in Washington, D.C., had kept the tissue samples. With the help of his friend, Joseph Gennaro, Wood examined the samples and compared them with octopus and squid tissue. Gennaro concluded that the tissues were *not* from a whale or squid, but were similar to existing octopuses. "The Florida Monster" was actually a giant octopus (*Octopus giganteus*)!

Wood calculated that the huge creature must have measured more than 180 feet in length with the tentacles extended when it was alive! Many experts believe that species of giant octopuses live in the deepest part of the Atlantic Ocean—the Puerto Rico Trench, 27,498 feet deep.

Although scientists have been unable to find additional evidence to support the existence of the giant octopus, that doesn't mean this huge creature isn't hidden in the ocean's depths. Until deep exploration dives for long periods of time are commonplace, the sea

will continue to hide its mysterious secrets
and the amazing creatures lurking within
it.

Sparky

Sparky, a 130-pound yellow Labrador retriever, loved going on walks with his master, John Culbertson. The early morning walk the big Lab took with his owner in January 1992 started out like all others in the six years they had been together. It was a cold winter day in Tullahoma, Tennessee, and although Sparky would have preferred to run and explore, he kept pace with his owner.

After the two had gone a short distance, Sparky sensed that something was wrong. Culbertson had stopped and seemed to be in distress. Suddenly, without warning, the big man became faint and collapsed to the ground. Before losing consciousness completely, he managed to slip his hand under Sparky's collar.

The yellow Lab couldn't wake up his owner. He licked his face and nudged him with his muzzle, but Culbertson didn't respond. Sparky realized that his master was in serious trouble. He decided to drag him home to get help. This was no easy task for the dog. His owner was a big man who weighed 227 pounds, an incredibly heavy weight for a dog to move.

Turning his body backward so the weight wouldn't pull at his chain collar and choke him, Sparky started dragging Culbertson home. Slowly but surely the Lab dragged his owner nearly two hundred yards to the front door of his house. He completed this difficult task just as Dorothy Culbertson stepped outside to look for her husband.

Seeing the exhausted dog and her unconscious husband, Dorothy immediately called an ambulance. Her fears were confirmed when doctors notified her that Culbertson had suffered a heart attack. Sparky's actions followed by immediate medical treatment probably saved his life.

John Culbertson later underwent triple bypass heart surgery and recovered from his heart attack. At his side was his faithful dog, Sparky.

"He saved my life, and he's worth millions to me," said Culbertson. "He's more of a friend than anything, and I will never never part with him."

Even as a frisky young pup, Sparky was special. He was raised by a neighbor, who also had a pet orangutan. When Culbertson developed a special attachment to the yellow Lab, his neighbor gave him the dog. Now the two are inseparable.

Sparky was named the Ken-L Ration Dog Hero of the Year for 1992. He received a certificate of merit, an engraved bowl, and a year's supply of Kibbles'n'Bits dog food. But what Sparky really cared about most was a pat and rub on the head from his master.

A special and mysterious bond exists between dogs and their owners. Loyalty, courage, and devotion are adjectives attributed more often to dogs than to any other creature.

Few would argue that the dog feels a wide range of emotions—from grief to anger to love. Many believe that the dog's attachment to humans is so strong it even exceeds the animal's own instinct for survival.

Man-Eating Plants

The trunk of the strange tree looked like an eight-foot-high pineapple sitting on its base. It was dark brown in color, and giant leaves attached at the top hung down to the ground. These huge leaves were thick and wide, and their outer surface was covered with sharp, hooked thorns.

A hole in the top of the tree was filled with a mysterious sweet liquid. Many hairy tendrils, which looked like the arms of an octopus, stretched out from the top in all directions but were motionless.

The natives surrounded the tree and forced one of their women to climb the leaves and stand at the peak. As the woman drank some of the liquid, the tree suddenly came to life. The green tendrils, one by one, wrapped their arms around her body, neck, and limbs. Like a nightmarish monster, the tendrils tightened their grip and strangled the life from their victim.

The woman's screams were reduced to quiet moans and then silence. As the giant leaves rose slowly in the air and enveloped her body, blood and fluid trickled down the trunk of the monstrous tree. The natives danced and cheered at the sight and drank the awful mixture. Ten days later, the leaves came down and nothing was left of the unfortunate woman except a skull at the foot of the tree.

Was this a scene from *Little Shop of Horrors*, the musical about a man-eating plant? Perhaps it was a clip from a late-night grade B horror movie? Guess again.

Based on an eyewitness description of a man-eating tree in Madagascar, which is an island off the coast of southeastern Africa, the incident was described in a letter written by Carle Liche, a German tourist. The letter was published in European scientific journals, magazines, and newspapers in the 1870s and 1880s.

Does this tree really exist? Many scientists believe it was a figment of the writer's

imagination. Though no specimen has been discovered supporting the existence of a man-eating tree, natives of Madagascar tell stories about the tree's existence. In fact, the belief in a man-eating tree or plant is common in southern Asia, including India.

Meat-eating plants do exist in nature. One example is the well-known Venus's flytrap, which feeds on the nutrients (mainly nitrogen) it gets from digesting insects. Its open leaves reveal a red center that secretes a liquid that smells like nectar. Insects are attracted to the color and smell.

Once the victim touches two of the sensitive trigger hairs, the open leaves flap shut and trap the prey inside. Digestive fluids slowly kill and dissolve the insect, and the flaps open again in a few days.

The Venus's flytrap is found mainly in North and South Carolina, and it feeds mostly on ants or flies. It will eat all meat and is capable of trapping and digesting even small frogs.

Another meat-eater is the pitcher plant, found in the southeastern part of the United States. Insects, attracted by the smell of nectar, stray into the pitcher-shaped hollow leaves of the plant. Thin hairs on the inside walls cause the insect to slip farther down into the hollow center until it reaches fluid at the bottom. There it drowns and begins to be digested by the plant.

Carnivorous, or meat-eating, plants are a unique and fascinating part of nature. Most people believe, however, that *man*-eating plants exist only in myths and stories. No one knows for sure. There are still many unexplored regions of the world, and these may yet reveal incredible, previously unknown mysteries.

Electric Eel

The local people of Calabozo, a small town in Venezuela, South America, had prepared a surprise for their guest. It was at the turn of the century, in the year 1800. The German scientist Baron von Humboldt was interested in the strange eels, native to the area, that produced electric current.

The townspeople were determined to provide von Humboldt with a live demonstration, along with some specimens. Although they didn't understand what electricity was, they knew this eel caused pain to animals and humans when they swam too close to it.

The locals herded several dozen horses into the swampland pools where the eels lived. The horses panicked and disturbed the eels, who started sending out electrical currents through the water.

Von Humboldt watched in fascination as some of the horses were stunned so badly they fell to their knees or drowned. The natives were able to capture several eels, which von Humboldt examined in detail and then later dissected.

The German scientist wanted to experience the electrical power of the eels firsthand, so he stood on the body of a live specimen. All at once, he felt a numbing pain throughout his body and then intense pain in his knees and joints as the eel shocked him.

Von Humboldt was responsible for the very first scientific account of the behavior of the electric eel. Well ahead of his time, he predicted that "electricity is the source of life and movement in all living things."

The electric eel has a thick, rounded body that ranges from six feet to about ten feet in length. Its eyes are very small, and one writer described its appearance as "looking like a child's unfinished clay animal." It lives in the swampy regions of northern South America.

The internal organs of the eel are contained in an area behind the head. The tail

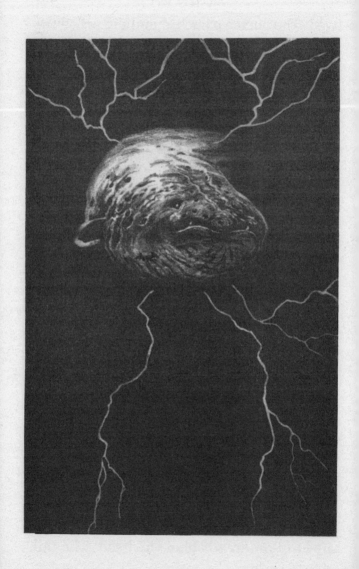

is where the electricity-producing organs of the eel are located. The tail is made up of thousands of sections, similar to cells in a battery. Just as any battery has a negative and positive end, the electric eel's head is positive, while the tail end is negative.

As the eel swims through the water, it sends out continuous weak electrical impulses. These impulses help guide it around obstacles and can also detect nearby prey. The eel uses its high-voltage capabilities to kill prey and for self-defense.

This amazing creature is capable of discharging up to six hundred volts at a time. That's enough power to light a dozen household bulbs! These high-voltage discharges can kill small fish and animals that the eel eats, and can stun large animals and even human beings. The danger to man lies in the possibility of drowning after being shocked.

Other species of electric fish include the electric catfish and the electric ray.

Nancy

Most incidents involving animals with mysterious and unexplained powers occur among household pets. Yet wild animals have also performed remarkable feats of extrasensory perception and intelligence. Take the case of a sea gull named Nancy described in the book *Psychic Animals* by Dennis Bardens.

Rachel Flynn and her sister, June, lived in Cape Cod, Massachusetts. Their home was a mile away from the ocean, and Rachel loved to walk on the rocky beaches and take in the beautiful New England scenery.

The two elderly sisters befriended one of the many sea gulls in the area. They fed it regularly and named the gull Nancy. Rachel and June looked forward to their daily visits with Nancy, and the bird seemed to return their friendship.

One day eighty-two-year-old Rachel was walking alone along the cliffs overlooking the ocean when she tripped and fell. She tumbled thirty feet down an embankment and landed on the beach below. She couldn't move and realized she must be seriously injured. Even worse, she lay trapped between two large rocks and wasn't easily visible from the cliff.

Thinking she would surely die, Rachel suddenly spotted a sea gull fluttering in the air above her.

Could it be Nancy? she thought. *Sea gulls all look alike, yet this one seems to be purposely staying near me.*

Out loud Rachel said, "For God's sake, Nancy, get help! Go! Get help!"

Sure enough, the bird flew away. "I probably scared it off," mumbled Rachel, who was in great pain by now, and she closed her eyes to rest.

What Rachel didn't know was that the bird flew directly to the Flynn house, where June was working in the kitchen. Nancy tapped on the window with her beak over and over again and flapped her wings.

"Shoo, Nancy, go away," said June, but the sea gull continued tapping.

"Leave, you silly bird," June snapped. "Don't bother me!"

After nearly fifteen minutes, June realized that the bird was trying to communicate with her. She went outside and said loudly, "What do you want, Nancy?" The gull flew a short distance and then stopped to be sure June would follow. The elderly woman walked as quickly as she could to try to keep up with the sea gull. She was a little frightened now because she hadn't seen Rachel in quite some time. June wondered if the gull's visit had something to do with her sister.

At last Nancy set down on the edge of the cliff. When June looked over, she searched the beach carefully and finally spotted her sister trapped below. "I'll get help, Rachel," she shouted down. "I'll be back soon. Hang on."

Rachel was hospitalized with an injured knee and severe cuts and bruises. June was positive that the bird had saved her sister's life.

How did the sea gull know Rachel needed help? It's too much of a coincidence for the bird to be flying in the exact location that the accident occurred. Did Nancy sense Rachel's distress and then fly to the scene?

What reasoning and thought processes did the bird use to fly back to the Flynn house and summon June by tapping on the window? What type of intelligent creature led the woman to her sister so she could get help?

When people use the term "birdbrain," they're referring to those with limited intelligence skills. Many scientists believe that birds are not capable of higher thoughts and reasoning. But don't tell that to Rachel Flynn, who owes her life to a birdbrain named Nancy.

Sea Serpents and Lake Monsters

It is a fact that large, mysterious, and unidentified animals live in the underwater depths of the world's lakes and oceans. The Loch Ness monster of Loch Ness in Scotland is the most famous.

For lack of a better name, this creature has been called a sea serpent or lake monster. For hundreds of years, men, women, and children have reported seeing it.

"It had a large, sharp snout and broad, large flippers," said a 1734 sighting.

"A great head and long neck rose out of the water . . . it had a series of humps," reported one 1905 sighting.

A 1915 sighting said, "It was about sixty

feet long ... and had four powerful paddle-like limbs."

A 1961 sighting stated, "We saw three humps, each about six feet long, and two near-side flippers come out of the water in a paddling motion."

"The creature was about seventy feet long. The head was large, the skin a dull brownish black in color," reported a sighting from 1965.

Descriptions often vary in the great number of reported sightings throughout the world. Yet there are several obvious similarities. This creature seems to be very large and has a long neck and flippers.

Some scientists have suggested this animal might be a giant eel or snake. But eels and snakes don't have the long neck or flippers reported in many sightings. Others insist it is a variety of long-neck seal or otter.

In another part of the world, in 1977, a Japanese trawler off the coast of New Zealand discovered the body of a thirty-foot-long creature in its nets. It had a long neck, four flippers, and weighed about four thousand pounds. The fisherman photographed, sketched, and measured the creature. Because it smelled so bad and was decomposing, the crew thought their catch of fresh fish would be spoiled. Unfortunately, they

threw the body back into the sea, thus depriving scientists of the chance to identify the creature.

From the photos and sketches, Japanese scientists concluded that it could have been a plesiosaur, a marine reptile extinct for 60 to 100 million years! Is it possible? After all, the prehistoric fish coelacanth, also thought to be extinct, was discovered alive and well in waters off southern Africa.

The Japanese scientists later changed their minds and concluded that the creature was the remains of a large basking shark. Without physical evidence, however, it's impossible to know for sure.

Many in the scientific community believe the plesiosaur is the answer to the reported sightings of sea serpents and lake monsters throughout the world. The plesiosaur had a long snakelike neck, a broad solid body, and four paddlelike legs. It ranged in size from ten to sixty feet.

The problem is, the plesiosaur was a saltwater reptile, and many of the sightings were made in very cold freshwater lakes. One theory states that long ago these areas were once part of the oceans that covered much of the Earth. Over the years, the water receded and the land emerged to cut off the lakes and trap the creatures within them from the sea.

The water changed slowly over time from salt to fresh, just as the temperatures changed from mild to very cold. The trapped plesiosaurs adapted slowly to these changes and still live in the depths today, coming to the surface occasionally.

Whatever they are, it is possible that these animals do exist. So many people have testified to their existence that it is almost impossible to pass them off as the result of an overactive imagination.

Are they giant eels, snakes, or seals? Are they living prehistoric reptiles from the Age of Dinosaurs? Are they serpents or monsters? Until a physical specimen is discovered and examined, the world can only wait and wonder.

Cunning Crows

The crows barely took notice of the farmer who waved his arms and tried to scare them away. The more the birds munched on the wheat, the more upset and frustrated the farmer became. He was determined not to let the crows destroy the crop that had taken him so long to grow.

The farmer hurried to his truck, reached for the rifle he kept under the seat, and mumbled out loud, "It's time to do a little crow hunting." As he got out of the truck, rifle in hand, and approached the birds, they spread their wings and took off instantly. It was as if the crows had warned each other, "He's got a gun now, let's get out of here."

The farmer scratched his head, got back into the truck, and drove off. Within minutes, the crows were back, eating the wheat as if nothing had happened.

This is a familiar scene to many farmers. Crows are considered to be the most intelligent of all birds. Were they reacting to the presence of the rifle itself or to the farmer's attitude, which changed once he got the rifle? It's difficult to determine the answer.

According to Jean Craighead George's book *Beastly Inventions*, a man named E. R. Kalmbach conducted an interesting experiment. He dressed in a long skirt and floppy hat that covered his face. Next, he hid a rifle in a hollow broomstick.

When Kalmbach got out of his car to face the crows, broomstick in hand, they flew away immediately. Later, he dressed exactly the same way but carried the broomstick without the rifle. Not only did he get out of his car, but he walked into the field. The crows didn't give him a second glance. They continued eating.

How did the crows know whether Kalmbach was armed and dangerous? Although birds possess the five senses of sight, hearing, touch, taste, and smell, their sense of sight has developed to a much greater degree than it has in other animals.

Could the crow's keen sense of sight have detected the rifle in the broomstick? That seems highly unlikely since no part of it was visible at any time. It's possible that the bird's sharp eyesight might have noticed certain movements of aggression and anger in the man that the crows recognized as danger.

Kalmbach was not consciously aware of changes in his body movements with or without the rifle. Yet, when he walked into the field with the weapon hidden in the broomstick, he was mentally thinking, "I'm going to kill some crows." This attitude might have caused minor changes in his walk and body movements that the crows were able to immediately sense.

If it wasn't the sharp eyesight of the crows that detected danger, was it something else that cannot be explained within the normal boundaries of the five senses? Could the crows have used ESP to determine if they were in danger?

Buffy

"I think we've found a beautiful spot to camp, Buffy," declared Mary Kearns to her pet keeshond. She chose a campsite in the valley near a small stream. It was an isolated clearing surrounded by small trees and bushes.

As Mary parked the car and began to unpack, she commented to the dog, "It's really lovely here. I hope I remembered to bring my camera."

Suddenly, Buffy ran to Mary and began barking in an odd unsettling way. As Mary carried supplies from the car to the campsite, the dog became more and more agitated.

"Take it easy, Buffy. What's bothering you?" asked Mary as she tried to calm down the anxious animal. But Buffy would not quiet down. His barking became wild and almost frightening.

Mary began to wonder whether camping here was such a good idea after all. The dog certainly didn't like this spot. His behavior seemed so strange that Mary's doubts about the place also grew.

She knew Buffy was a special dog. He always seemed to know about things before they happened. She remembered how Buffy would bark and get excited before her daughter came to visit.

"Okay, Buffy, you win," declared Mary out loud to the keeshond. "I think it would be better if we found another place." Mary repacked the car and drove a distance until she located another pretty camping spot, this time on a hillside.

"I think this is an even lovelier spot than before," she exclaimed. "What a fabulous view of the area!" Buffy, who had completely calmed down, licked his owner's hand and curled up at her feet. After a good dinner and a short walk, Mary and Buffy settled down for the night.

Up early after a restful sleep, Mary broke camp, repacked her gear, and began traveling again. Passing through a nearby town, she bought a local paper and saw some shocking news. The headline read "THREE CAMPERS DROWNED IN FLASH FLOOD."

The newspaper article described how an unexpected rainstorm high in the mountains caused a flash flood. The water roared down a valley without warning, killing the unfortunate campers. It was the exact valley where she and Buffy had first stopped to camp!

How had Buffy known there was something wrong? Can animals sense danger before it happens? Did Buffy know he and his owner would be drowned in a flash flood if they camped in the valley that night? Or was it by chance that the keeshond became so upset?

A precognitive warning or a coincidence? Mary Kearns is convinced that Buffy's powers of extrasensory perception saved her life.

Spiders on the Loose

"It's an ugly bug. Kill it quickly!" screams a girl as a common household spider scurries across the carpet of her house. After it's crushed with a tissue and deposited in the garbage can, the girl heaves a sigh of relief. "Spiders are so creepy and disgusting! I hate them."

People fear and dislike spiders mainly because of the way they look and act. They have eight long legs, move fast, hide in dark corners, and spin sticky webs that trap bugs. They may not be lovable little creatures, but they control the number of insects in the house and garden. They're a benefit to mankind even if people don't appreciate them.

There are thirty thousand species of spiders in the world, some of which live fascinating lives. Just imagine the South American bird-eating spider. With a ten-inch leg span, it's the largest of them all!

One type of spider spends its entire life underwater, yet it still breathes oxygen. The water spider spins silk and attaches it to an underwater plant. Then the spider returns to the surface and traps an air bubble with its body. The bubble is released under the silk to form an air pocket shaped like a tiny bell. After several more trips to the surface for more air, the spider's home is complete. When the oxygen supply gets low, the spider rises again for more air.

The fishing or diving spider is comfortable on land as well as water. It walks or floats on the surface of the water using an air bubble held beneath its body. Resting on plant leaves, this spider dangles its front legs in the water. In this way, it attracts insects and, in some cases, very small fish and tadpoles to eat. When frightened, the fishing spider dives several inches beneath the surface and can stay underwater for up to an hour!

The web-throwing spider spins a net and holds it with its legs. The spider then hangs upside down from a plant or branch. It waits

for prey to pass underneath and casts the net on unsuspecting insects.

The bolas spider is named after the Spanish weapon used to lasso or rope cattle. A bola is a long cord or thong with heavy balls at the end. This spider manufactures its own special bola to catch prey.

The bolas attaches a single horizontal silk line to the bottom of a branch or twig. The spider then spins a second line that hangs down vertically from the first. At the end of the second line, the spider attaches a sticky gumlike substance in the shape of a small ball.

Hanging from the first line, the spider uses several of its legs to grasp and control the second line. Just as a cowboy might use a lasso or bola to snare cattle, this spider swings the line to catch insects. The spider aims carefully so the ball at the end of the line hits the prey and sticks to it. Before the unfortunate victim can free itself, the spider rushes in for the kill.

Of the thousands of species of spiders that exist, only about a dozen are really dangerous to man. Of these, the black widow is the best known. It only bites in self-defense but is capable of killing an animal thousands of times its size.

Scientists wonder why the small black

widow spider, which captures prey from its web, also possesses a bite more powerful than rattlesnake venom. It's actually more dangerous to male spiders than to people, for after mating, the black widow often eats the male!

Dolphins to
the Rescue

No woman had ever swum the fifteen-mile channel called Cook Strait in New Zealand. Lynne Cox, a long-distance swimmer, wanted to be the first. She knew it would be difficult, but she never expected it to be so dangerous.

It wasn't the distance that bothered her. When Lynne was fourteen, she swam from the California coast to Catalina Island, twenty-seven miles in all. It took her twelve hours and thirty-six minutes under good weather conditions and in a calm sea.

Swimming through Cook Strait was a little like traveling through a hurricane. The winds were up to forty-five knots and the waves were six to eight feet high. The boat that always accompanied Lynne on her swims was having trouble just staying afloat.

Lynne was getting very tired fighting the waves and weather. Despite shouts of encouragement from her trainer in the boat, the cold and exhaustion finally got to her. Lynne felt she couldn't go any farther.

Suddenly, just as she was about to quit the swim and signal the boat to pick her up, Lynne found herself surrounded by forty to fifty dolphins. It was as if the dolphins wanted to help her keep going.

"I started feeling better," said Lynne, "and concentrated on watching the dolphins instead of my own tiredness and the weather. After an hour, they left and another group of dolphins joined me. They were squeaking and clicking all around me. Some were so close that I could have reached out and touched them.

"The dolphins had perfect timing," Lynne explained. "They came when I was feeling bad and cheered me up. It was wonderful." She adds, "They guided me right in to the finish!"

Did the dolphins sense that Lynne was in trouble and about to give up? Did they purposely swim with her, or was it just a coincidence that they came at that particular moment?

Some people think that dolphins are not only extremely intelligent creatures but have a special psychic ability beyond the normal five senses. Most people agree that there is a unique link between dolphins and man. They have attacked sharks but they have never attacked people. In fact, there are numerous stories on record that dolphins have helped or rescued people from drowning.

In one report, a drowning woman was pushed to shore by a dolphin. Another swimmer was having trouble with muscle cramps. A dolphin swam up under him and kept him afloat until the cramps passed. Still another swimmer became disoriented and panicked in the water, unable to find his way back to his boat. A dolphin appeared to guide him out of trouble.

How could the dolphins know these people were in peril? And if the creatures sensed danger, how did they know what to do to solve the problem?

There are those who believe that dolphins

use telepathic ability to read people's minds. Others say they are friendly, intelligent, and playful animals who just happen to show up at the right time.

Is it a coincidence or telepathy? Someday scientists may discover the truth.

Forever Friends

Cats, more than other animals, are said to possess mysterious unexplained powers. Perhaps it's their independence and reserved nature that make people uncertain about cats—and in some cases, even afraid of them.

Whereas dogs are referred to as "man's best friend," cats are often seen as creatures of magic and the supernatural. They're portrayed unfairly by several commonly held beliefs and superstitions. It's said that witches take the form of black cats when they want to move freely and undetected among people. It's no coincidence that, at Halloween, black cat costumes and decorations are nearly as popular as ghosts and jack-o'-lanterns. This discomfort and uncertainty about felines have contributed to making the black cat a symbol of bad luck for superstitious people all year long!

Yet cats often have proven themselves to be just as faithful, obedient, and loyal as any other animal. Take the case of the cat named Bill. Bill and his owner shared a special relationship that only came from years of living together. They knew and understood each other's gestures, moods, habits, and body language.

One day, Bill was left at home while his master went on a short trip. It wasn't unusual for the cat to stay behind on these occasions. There was plenty of food, a litter box, and even a slightly open window so Bill could go in and out.

The days passed, and Bill's owner did not return home. He had been badly hurt in a train accident and died a few days later. The funeral took place in a cemetery near the hospital in which he had died.

The man's brother had made the funeral arrangements in a hurry. With everything else on his mind, he had completely forgotten about the cat. During the graveside service he was amazed to see Bill there. The cat had somehow known what had happened to his owner and traveled to the cemetery to pay his last respects to his beloved master.

After the service, the brother quietly watched as the cat walked slowly to the edge of the open grave and looked down at the coffin. After a few moments, Bill turned and slowly made his way home. There was no question in the brother's mind that the animal was suffering the loss of its master and friend.

Did the cat sense his owner's accident and death? How could Bill have known where the funeral was being held and when?

Whatever guided the cat to the funeral of his master, it's apparent Bill possessed two important qualities we all wish for in our animals as well as our friends—love and loyalty.

Chimp Talk

In the late 1960s, two teachers named Beatrix and Allen Gardner raised a young chimpanzee as if it were a human child. The Gardners did not believe that a chimp could imitate human speech, so they taught it sign language instead.

The chimp, named Washoe, eventually learned to use more than 132 signs. Dorothy Hinshaw Patent, in her book *How Smart Are Animals*, described how Washoe would sign "Baby mine" for her doll and "Listen dog" when a dog barked. She even invented her own new sign for the bib she wore.

Once Washoe asked one of her trainers, Roger Fouts, for some fruit. "Fruit me," she requested. Roger replied in sign language, "Sorry but I not have any fruit." Washoe wasn't pleased with this response and signed back "Dirty Roger." The chimp made up her own insult and used it to express her anger.

In another conversation with a human trainer, Washoe asked for an orange. When he replied, "No more orange, what you want?" the chimp again asked for an orange. When the trainer gave the same response, Washoe signed, "You go car gimme orange. Hurry!" The chimp remembered that people drove in cars to buy food at stores, although she hadn't been in one for two years.

There have been many successful language experiments with animals. In the 1970s a gorilla named Koko was taught over five hundred signs. Koko was able to make statements using three to six signs at once.

An orangutan named Chantek, in addition to knowing more than one hundred signs, learned to work for tokens to use toward rewards later on. If Chantek cleaned her room, she got a certain number of tokens and could exchange them for treats.

A pigmy chimpanzee named Kanzi was taught to communicate with symbols on a computer keyboard. He also learned to understand spoken English commands.

The question is, could these animals really

have understood language? It seemed so, yet
scientists have expressed many doubts about
these experiments. Some have said that
when people are involved in reading signs
made by chimps or gorillas, there is room for
error in their interpretations. Perhaps un-
consciously the people are interpreting a
sign they want to see. Therefore, the success
of these studies is difficult to judge.

Other scientists say the intention of the
speaker is the key to understanding language. When a chimp signs "Orange," does it
mean "I have a desire for an orange" or does
it just know that the sign for orange will result in getting an orange? According to Dorothy Hinshaw Patent: "The difficult thing is
finding out whether an animal is using symbols consciously or just performing behavior
that will get rewards."

Didn't Washoe reveal an understanding
and intelligence beyond that of simple mem-
orization when she created her own word for
her bib or made up an insult? Some scientists don't believe it does. They simply do not
feel these animals have enough intelligence
to put words together to form sentences or
thoughts.

They point to the fact that few of the animals showed creativity in their language
use. Whereas even a young child can enjoy

stories and make up fantasies, these animals only spoke about real things they had contact with.

Such criticism of ape and chimp language research has led to large cuts in funding in this area. This is unfortunate, since there is much to be learned about the way animals think and feel and how they communicate with humans as well as other animals.

Someday we may discover whether animals can learn and understand human language. But there are those who would prefer not to know. As Patent states: "Perhaps it is difficult for some people to let go of the notion that language is the one thing that makes humans unique."

Strulli

"Let's go for a walk, Strulli," said Josef Becker to his German shepherd. According to Dennis Bardens, in his book *Psychic Animals*, the dog and master often went for a late afternoon stroll, usually ending up at the local inn. This particular day was no exception. Josef brought the dog inside with him, sat down, and ordered refreshments.

Josef began talking to some friends when suddenly the big dog started howling at his master. Strulli tugged at Josef's clothes and tried to drag him out of his seat. When Josef resisted, Strulli continued howling and started running around in circles.

"What is wrong with you today?" Josef

asked the usually well-behaved animal. "If you can't sit quietly, you'll have to leave!

"Back in a second, fellows," he said to his friends as he walked the dog outside, then ducked back into the inn, shutting the door behind him. "Now where was I?" asked Josef as he returned to his food and companions.

Within seconds, Strulli came through another open door and began tugging again at his master's clothes. "Looks like your dog doesn't want you to stay, Josef," said one of the men. "You won't have any peace with him carrying on like that."

"I'm sorry, boys," he apologized. "Something's bothering the dog, and I'll just have to find out what it is. I'll be back another time."

As Josef left the inn with Strulli, he glanced at his watch and saw that it was two minutes before five. They had barely been walking a couple of minutes when there was a deafening explosion behind him on the street.

Turning around, Josef was horrified to see that the inn had collapsed. Timber, bricks, and plaster had crashed down on the friends he had just left behind. Twenty people were injured and nine people were killed in the accident.

A shocked Josef turned slowly to face his

dog. "My god, Strulli, you knew, didn't you?" The man knelt down and held the pet close to him.

Did the German shepherd have a premonition of disaster? How could the dog have known something bad was going to happen? Not until much later was it discovered that builders next door had unknowingly damaged the inn's foundations, causing a weakening and the eventual collapse of the structure.

What special sensitivity and perception do dogs and other animals possess that enable them to have knowledge of future events? Too often, unexplained animal behavior is routinely ignored by calling it "instinct." Is it instinct to know the future or is it ESP? Do dogs have certain psychic abilities?

Next time your dog unexpectedly tugs at your clothing to get you to move, will you sit tight or will you follow? There's no doubt what Josef Becker will do.

Glossary

AGGRESSION: attack, fight.

AGITATED: excited, frantic, wild.

ALKALOIDS: organic substances that contain nitrogen and can neutralize acids; some are very poisonous.

ANTICOAGULANT: stops blood from clotting.

APHID: an insect that sucks the juice from plants.

ASTEROID: small rocky objects in orbit around the sun.

ATTRIBUTE: belonging to, characteristic.

AUTOPSY: examination and dissection of a dead body to determine the cause of death.

BOMBARDIER: someone who operates a bomb sight and releases bombs.

CANINE: dog.

CARCASS: body, remains, corpse.

CARNIVOROUS: flesh- or meat-eating.

CHITIN: hard outer covering of insects.

CLAIRVOYANCE: the ability to identify or become aware of an object, person, or event without using the five basic senses (sight, hearing, smell, taste, and touch).

COINCIDENCE: occurrence or event that seems related to another but is not actually connected.

CONFIRM: approve, verify.

CONGESTED: clogged, overcrowded.

CRYPTOZOOLOGY: the study of hidden, unidentified living animals.

CURATOR: the person in charge of a museum, zoo, library, or other exhibit.

DEBRIS: wreckage, rubbish.

DECOMPOSE: decay, rot.

DISSECT: cut open, examine.

DISTRESS: difficulty, pain, anguish.

EMBANKMENT: rise or slope on a hillside.

EVENTUAL: expected, approaching.

EXCEED: go beyond, outdo, pass.

EXTINCT: dead, vanished.

EXTRASENSORY PERCEPTION (ESP): special abilities and knowledge that extend beyond the normal five senses.

FELINE: cat.
FEROCIOUS: violent, fierce.
FIGMENT: fantasy, made up.
FILLY: female horse, mare.
FLOUNDERING: struggling awkwardly.
FOSSIL: remains, skeleton.

GROOVE: slot, opening.
GUILLOTINE: a sharp-bladed machine used to cut off a person's head.

HERBIVOROUS: grass- or plant-eating.
HESITANT: unsure, reluctant.

IMITATE: copy, duplicate.
IMPULSE: a drive or force pushing a person or event forward.
INTERPRETATION: translation, explanation.

LARVA: an insect in the earliest stage of development.
LASSO: rope, snare.

MALNUTRITION: improper diet, undernourishment.
MAMMALS: human beings and animals that

feed mother's milk to their young and have skin covered with hair.

METEORITE: object from space, varying in size, that does not burn itself out in the Earth's atmosphere like a meteor but hits the Earth instead.

MUZZLE: snout, nose.

NEMATOCYST: stinging cells of jellyfish.

NOCTURNAL: active during the night.

NUDGE: gently push, shove.

PARANORMAL: not able to be explained by science.

PARASITE: a plant or animal that lives off another, giving nothing in return.

PENETRATE: enter, spread through.

PERCEPTION: understanding, awareness.

PERIL: danger, threat.

PHENOMENON: an extraordinary or unusual occurrence.

PHEROMONES: substances secreted by bees and other animals that change behavior; alarm pheromones make bees aggressive and attack in mass.

POLLINATION: transfer of pollen from the male to the female part of flowers and plants, which makes fruit and vegetable production possible.

POTENT: strong, powerful.

PRECOGNITION: the knowledge of events before they actually happen; the ability to see the future.

PREDATOR: an animal or person that destroys, robs, or eats greedily.

PREMONITION: an advance warning of an event; similar to precognition.

PREY: game, catch, target.

PRIMITIVE: crude, simple, ancient, from earliest times.

PSI-TRAILING: orientation by unexplained means.

PSYCHIC: sensitive to supernatural forces.

RECEDE: move back, withdraw.

REINCARNATION: the belief that a person's soul is reborn in a new bodily form after death.

ROE DEER: type of small European and Asiatic deer.

RUBBLE: wreckage, rubbish.

SCALES: outer protective covering of fish or reptiles.

SECRETE: ooze, drip.

SERRATED: sharp, sawlike notches on an edge.

SKEPTICAL: doubtful, uncertain.

SNARE: catch, trap, entangle.

SNOUT: nose, beak.

SPECIES: a single, distinct kind of plant or animal.

SPECIMEN: a sample.

SPORES: reproductive organs produced by mosses and ferns.

STALK: pursue or approach under cover.

SUCCESSION: in order, series.

SUPERNATURAL: anything caused by other than the known forces of nature.

SUPERSTITION: belief based on stories or myths, not necessarily true.

TELEPATHY: the ability to communicate over any distance from one mind to another without actually speaking.

TENDRILS: thin, armlike parts of a climbing plant that coil around or cling to something.

TENTACLES: long, thin, armlike extensions of octopus or squid used for grabbing or feeling.

TOKEN: similar to a coin that can be exchanged for something of value.

TRAWLER: a boat that drags along a large net to catch fish on the bottom.

UNIQUE: one of a kind, unequaled.

VENOM: poison.

Bibliography

Books

Allaby, Michael, and Lovelock, James. *The Great Extinction*. Garden City, N.Y.: Doubleday, 1983.

Bakker, Robert T. *The Dinosaur Heresies*. New York: William Morrow and Company, 1986.

Bardens, Dennis. *Psychic Animals*. New York: Henry Holt and Company, 1987.

Boone, J. Allen. *Kinship With All Life*. New York: Harper and Brothers, 1954.

Bronson, Wilfrid S. *Beetles*. New York: Harcourt, Brace and World, Inc., 1963.

Burton, Maurice, and Burton, Robert. *Encyclopedia of Fish*. London, Eng.: Octopus Books Limited, 1975.

Compton, Gail. "What Is the World's Deadliest Animal?"
In *Maneaters and Marmosets*. New York: Hearst
Books, 1976.

Constable, George. *Mysterious Creatures*. Richmond, Va.:
Time-Life Books, 1988.

Cousteau, Jacques-Yves, and Diole', Philippe. *Octopus
and Squid*. Garden City, N.Y.: Doubleday, 1973.

Dinsdale, Tim. *Monster Hunt*. Washington, D.C.: Acropo-
lis Books, 1972.

Dozier, Thomas A. *Dangerous Sea Creatures*. New York:
Time-Life Films, 1977.

George, Jean Craighead. *Beastly Inventions*. New York:
David McKay Company, 1970.

Henry, Thomas R. *The Strangest Things in the World*.
Washington, D.C.: Public Affairs Press, 1958.

Hitchings, Thomas, editor-in-chief. *Facts on File*. New
York: Facts on File, Inc., 1991.

Jenkinson, Michael. *Beasts Beyond the Fire*. New York:
E. P. Dutton, 1980.

Key, Alexander. *The Strange White Dove*. Philadelphia:
Westminster Press, 1972.

Mackal, Roy P. *Searching for Hidden Animals*. Garden
City, N.Y.: Doubleday, 1980.

Matthews, Rupert. *Monster Mysteries*. New York: The
Bookwright Press, 1989.

Matthiessen, Peter. *Blue Meridian*. New York: Random House, 1971.

McFarland, Kevin. *Incredible!* New York: Hart Publishing Company, 1976.

Neary, John. *Insects and Spiders*. Richmond, Va.: Time-Life Books, 1977.

Patent, Dorothy Hinshaw. *How Smart Are Animals*. San Diego, Calif.: Harcourt Brace Jovanovich, Publishers, 1990.

Potter, Anthony. *The Killer Bees*. New York: Grosset and Dunlap, 1977.

Preston-Mafham, Rod, and Preston-Mafham, Ken. *Spiders of the World*. New York: Facts on File Publications, 1984.

Pringle, Laurence. *Batman—Exploring the World of Bats*. New York: Charles Scribner's Sons, 1991.

———*Killer Bees*. New York: Morrow Junior Books, 1990.

Reader's Digest Association. *Strange Stories, Amazing Facts*. Pleasantville, N.Y.: The Reader's Digest Association, Inc., 1976.

Steiger, Brad, and Steiger, Sherry Hansen. *Strange Powers of Pets*. New York: Donald I. Fine, 1992.

Stokes, Donald W. *A Guide to the Behavior of Common Birds*. Boston: Little, Brown and Company, 1979.

Taylor, David. *Animal Monsters*. Minneapolis, Minn.: Lerner Publications Company, 1989.

Thomson, Keith Stewart. *Living Fossil*. New York: W. W. Norton and Company, 1991.

Tributsch, Helmut. *When the Snakes Awake*. Cambridge, Mass.: The MIT Press, 1982.

Weyer, Edward M., Jr. *Strangest Creatures on Earth*. New York: Sheridan House, 1953.

Wylder, Joseph. *Psychic Pets*. New York: Stonehill Publishing, 1978.

Periodicals

"Sam's Incredible Journey of Love." *Weekly World News*. May 3, 1983.

"The Dog Who Walked Through Fire." *Reader's Digest*. April 1982.

Miscellaneous

Winner's Press Releases, Ken-L Ration Dog Hero of the Year—1992 Program, c/o McDowell and Piasecki, Chicago, Illinois.